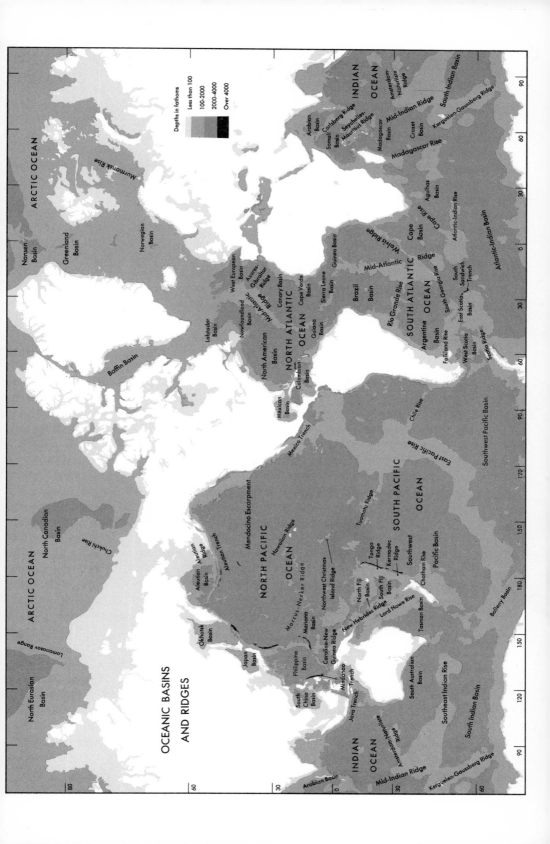

OCEANIC BASINS AND RIDGES

Depths in fathoms
- Less than 100
- 100-2000
- 2000-4000
- Over 4000

ARCTIC OCEAN

ARCTIC OCEAN

North Eurasian Basin

Lomonosov Range

North Canadian Basin

Chukchi Rise

Okhotsk Basin

Japan Basin

Philippine Basin

South China Basin

Mindanao Trench

Java Trench

Caroline-New Guinea Ridge

Mariana Basin

Marcus-Necker Ridge

Aleutian Basin

Aleutian Ridge

Aleutian Trench

Mendocino Escarpment

NORTH PACIFIC OCEAN

Hawaiian Ridge

Northwest Christmas Island Ridge

North Fiji Basin

New Hebrides Ridge

South Fiji Basin

Tonga Ridge

Kermadec Ridge

Tuamotu Ridge

Southwest Pacific Basin

Southwest Pacific Basin

Chatham Rise

SOUTH PACIFIC OCEAN

Lord Howe Rise

Tasman Basin

South Australian Basin

INDIAN OCEAN

Arabian Basin

Mid-Indian Ridge

Amsterdam-Naturliste Ridge

Kerguelen-Gausberg Ridge

Southeast Indian Rise

South Indian Basin

South Indian Basin

Balleny Basin

East Pacific Rise

Chile Rise

Mexico Trench

Mexican Basin

Colombian Basin

Guiana Basin

NORTH ATLANTIC OCEAN

North American Basin

Newfoundland Basin

Labrador Basin

Baffin Basin

West European Basin

Azores-Gibraltar Ridge

Mid-Atlantic Ridge

Canary Basin

Cape Verde Basin

Sierra Leone Basin

Guinea Basin

Brazil Basin

Rio Grande Rise

Argentine Basin

Falkland Rise

West Scotia Basin

East Scotia Basin

Scotia Ridge

South Sandwich Trench

South Georgia Rise

SOUTH ATLANTIC OCEAN

Mid-Atlantic Ridge

Walvis Ridge

Cape Basin

Cape Rise

Agulhas Basin

Atlantic-Indian Rise

Atlantic-Indian Basin

Greenland Basin

Nansen Basin

Norwegian Basin

Murmansk Rise

INDIAN OCEAN

Arabian Basin

Somali Basin

Carlsberg Ridge

Seychelles-Mauritius Ridge

Madagascar Basin

Mid-Indian Ridge

Crozet Basin

Madagascar Rise

Amsterdam-Naturliste Ridge

South Indian Basin

Kerguelen-Gausberg Ridge

Oceans

Karl K. Turekian

Yale University

Prentice-Hall, Inc.,   Englewood Cliffs, New Jersey

Design by Walter Behnke

Illustrations by Vincent Kotschar

PRENTICE-HALL INTERNATIONAL, INC., *London*

PRENTICE-HALL OF AUSTRALIA, PTY., LTD., *Sydney*

PRENTICE-HALL OF CANADA, LTD., *Toronto*

PRENTICE-HALL OF INDIA PVT. LTD., *New Delhi*

PRENTICE-HALL OF JAPAN, INC., *Tokyo*

Current printing (last digit):
10 9 8 7 6 5 4 3 2 1

FOUNDATIONS OF EARTH SCIENCE SERIES

A. Lee McAlester, Editor

C

Foundations
of Earth Science Series

Elementary Earth Science textbooks have too long reflected mere traditions in teaching rather than the triumphs and uncertainties of present-day science. In geology, the time-honored textbook emphasis on geomorphic processes and descriptive stratigraphy, a pattern begun by James Dwight Dana over a century ago, is increasingly anachronistic in an age of shifting research frontiers and disappearing boundaries between long-established disciplines. At the same time, the extraordinary expansions in exploration of the oceans, atmosphere, and interplanetary space within the past decade have made obsolete the unnatural separation of the "solid Earth" science of geology from the "fluid Earth" sciences of oceanography, meteorology, and planetary astronomy, and have emphasized the need for authoritative introductory textbooks in these vigorous subjects.

Stemming from the conviction that beginning students deserve to share in the excitement of modern research, the *Foundations of Earth Science Series* has been planned to provide brief, readable, up-to-date introductions to all aspects of modern Earth science. Each volume has been written by an authority on the subject covered, thus insuring a first-hand treatment seldom found in introductory textbooks. Four of the volumes—*Structure of the Earth, Earth Materials, The Surface of the Earth,* and *Earth Resources*—cover topics traditionally taught in physical geology courses. Three volumes—*Geologic Time, Ancient Environments,* and *The History of Life*—treat historical topics, and the remaining three volumes—*Oceans, The Atmosphere,* and *The Solar System*—deal with the "fluid Earth sciences" of oceanography, meteorology, and astronomy. Each volume, however, is complete in itself and can be combined with other volumes in any sequence, thus allowing the teacher great flexibility in course arrangement. In addition, these compact and inexpensive volumes can be used individually to supplement and enrich other introductory textbooks.

Acknowledgements

The author would like to thank: his wife, who has tolerated many discussions on the content of this book; Mrs. Nancy Cott, who has transcribed illegible script into a comprehensible typed manuscript; and Ronald Nelson, of Prentice-Hall, who helped improve the clarity of expression.

Contents

Introduction

Ours is the only planet in the Solar System with sufficient surface water to form oceans. Because 71 per cent of the Earth is covered by water, the study of the oceans is fundamental to our understanding of the Earth. The discipline concerned with oceanic processes is called oceanography, but oceanic processes are so numerous and varied that the science of oceanography is usually further subdivided into four main areas: physical oceanography, which deals with the properties of ocean water in motion; chemical oceanography, which is concerned with the chemical reactions occurring in the oceans; biological oceanography, which includes the study of life in the oceans; and geological oceanography, which is concerned with the structure of the ocean bottom and the processes active there. In the following chapters we will be exploring, principally, the geology and chemistry of the oceans, both present and past. In order to understand these aspects adequately, we will also have to discuss, in less detail, the circulation of the oceans and the role of biological activity in the seas. Before going on to *what* we know of the oceans today, it will be useful to review *why* this knowledge was obtained—

that is, practical as well as scientific reasons that have made the study of the oceans so compelling to scientists and explorers alike.

In the first place, the entire history of the Earth is linked closely to the oceans. The oceans receive the burdens of streams derived from the weathering and erosion of the land. This debris, accumulating on the ocean floor as sediments, records the history of geologic events and preserves, as fossils, a representation of the changing life of the seas.

The oceans also regulate major processes occurring on the Earth's surface. They are the primary source of water that reaches the continents as rain and snow, and they contain the largest reservoir of carbon which is involved in the biological cycle. The high heat capacity of water makes the oceans an important regulator of climate, especially in maritime lands. And the movements of its currents are of fundamental importance for both marine life and man.

The swarming, diversified life of the sea has been an important source of food for man through the ages. Molluscs, crustaceans, fishes, whales, and seaweed are, today, major resources for large parts of the world. In addition, non-food products derived from the animals and plants of the sea have various economic uses, ranging from pearls to building materials.

The chemical resources of ocean water of interest to man include fresh water obtained by desalination and elements for industrial products such as magnesium, potassium, bromine, and iodine. Diamond accumulations on some sea coasts, offshore oil and gas, and phosphate and manganese deposited from the ocean itself round out the list of useful products from the sea.

Aside from the chemical and biological products of the sea, the economic utilization of the oceans extends into the areas of communications and transportation. Transoceanic cables are laid on sediments that may be subject to slumping or distortion as the result of earthquakes and other events. These movements of the sediment may break or disrupt the cables causing costly delays and repairs. For this reason, among others, the topography, earthquake activity, and sedimentary properties of the ocean bottom are studied in great detail. Ships sailing on the surface of the ocean provide the most obvious practical use of the sea, but the increased use of submarines for exploratory, military, and possibly commercial purposes have aroused renewed interest in the properties of deep water. Underwater navigation and remote sensing by sonar have become important for military as well as commercial reasons, hence, the variations in physical and chemical properties of ocean water with geography and depth are part of today's intense oceanographic efforts.

For all these practical reasons as well as the perennial scientific quests of the hows and whys, the sea has become an area of intense study, especially since World War II. The range of techniques available, the number of oceanic research ships, and the number of qualified scientists have all increased tremendously in the past 25 years. The findings of these oceanographers as well as those of the early pioneers will be discussed in the following chapters.

1

Topography and structure

of ocean basins

The ocean basins are not merely inert receptacles for water and continental debris. Rather, the topography and structure of the ocean bottom are highly variable from place to place and reflect processes in the Earth's interior. These features also vary in permanence so that the ocean bottom of today may not be like the ocean bottom of 50 million years ago. In this chapter we will survey what has been learned of the topography and structure of ocean basins, mainly as the result of intensive studies during the last 25 years.

Ocean-Bottom Topography

For determining the major topographic features of the ocean bottom, some sort of remote sensing device is required. Shallow water depths were determined in the past by means of a *sounding line* made of hemp with a lead weight attached, (hence the phrase "plumbing the depths" from the Latin *plumbum* for lead). In the latter part of the nineteenth cen-

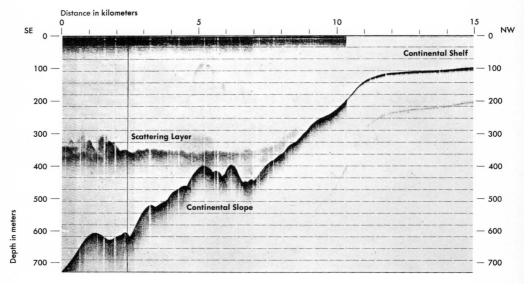

Figure 1–1 *Precision echo sounding across the continental margin off Virginia. The record shows the transition from the nearly horizontal smooth surface of the outer continental shelf to the inclined irregular surface of the upper continental slope. Reflections from a deep scattering layer within the ocean are visible between 300 and 400 meters below sea level. The scattering layer is believed to be due to certain organisms. Vertical exaggeration is about 12:1 so that the true inclination of the upper continental slope is about 6° from horizontal. (Courtesy Peter A. Rona, Hudson Laboratories of Columbia University.)*

tury, hemp gave way to metal wire, and until about 1920 soundings were obtained in all parts of the oceans by this method. In shallow waters, soundings could be made relatively rapidly, but in the deep ocean, where the average depth is 4,000 meters, it would take several hours to lower and raise the sounding line. When research vessels began to dredge the deep ocean depths in the latter part of the nineteenth century the length of cable required to lower the dredge to the ocean bottom gave additional depth information. Similarly, deepwater sampling programs could be used for determining depth at the location of sampling. It is evident that gathering data on depth distribution in the oceans was a long, tedious, and spotty endeavor when these methods were employed. Nevertheless, by 1920 enough soundings had been obtained to indicate the elementary fact that the deep ocean bottom is not a featureless plain and to permit the cataloging of the distribution of depths at sea.

After 1920, although the sounding-line method continued to be used in oceanographic programs, *echo sounders* began to be developed. This technique depends on generating a sound signal that is transmitted through the water, reflected off the bottom as an echo, and received aboard the ship generating the signal. Since the velocity of sound is a function of the temperature, salinity, and pressure of the water, these properties must be known or approximated in order to translate the transit time of the signal into depth. During World War II these techniques were immensely improved, and since then all soundings have been made with continuously operating, precision depth-recorders that give bottom profiles of the type seen in Fig. 1–1.

Methods of navigation have also improved considerably since the war, thus permitting the accurate location of ocean-bottom features. Standard celestial and solar navigation is still a major means of getting accurate fixes of location. But since this method requires a precise measurement of the distance of a heavenly body above the horizon, overcast skies are a hindrance. In such cases a ship is forced to proceed by dead reckoning based on the position calculated from the last astronomic fix. Accuracy is diminished because of ocean currents and drift due to winds. Now, however, at least within transmitting distances from land, a form of electronic triangulation called LORAN can be used in all weather, permitting an accuracy of less than one kilometer. Currently, too, a growing number of ships are using signals from artificial satellites for the accurate determination of location. This method is particularly important in remote areas of heavy overcast skies, such as the Antarctic, because a purely electronic signal from a precisely known source is used in establishing location.

The results of the very large number of soundings made of the ocean bottom indicate that there are three major topographic features common to all oceans: *the continental margins, the ocean-basin floors,* and the major *oceanic ridge systems* (Fig. 1–2). In addition to these major features there are additional ridges and rises which occur throughout the ocean basins. The major topographic systems mentioned above, combined with these secondary ridges and rises, break up the oceans into a group of smaller basins. The geography of these subdivisions is shown in the map on the first page of the book.

FIGURE 1–2   *The major topographic features of the ocean bottom. (After Heezen, Tharp, and Ewing, 1959.)*

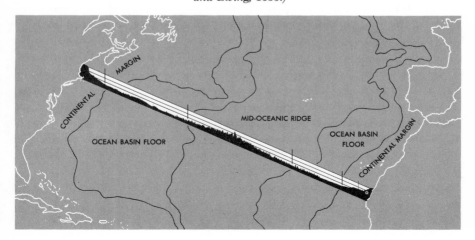

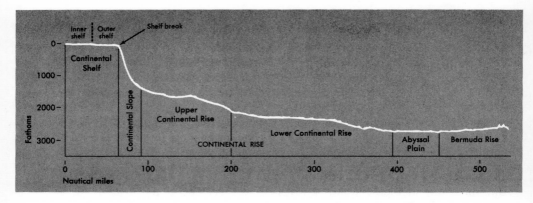

FIGURE 1–3 *The continental margin province divisions as typified by the northeastern United States. A fathom is equal to 6 feet or 1.82 meters. (After Heezen, Tharp, and Ewing, 1959.)*

The Continental Margin

The continental margin is commonly composed of either of two sequences proceeding seaward: shelf-slope-rise (as in Fig. 1–3) or shelf-slope-trench-ridge. The *continental shelf* is the submerged continuation of the topography and geology visible on the adjacent land, modified in part by marine erosion or sediment deposition. The *shelf break*, wherever it can be seen unambiguously, marks the seaward extent of the continental shelf and occurs at depths of between 10 to 500 meters, averaging 200 meters. The relief on the shelf is generally less than 20 meters. The *continental slope*, the next seaward feature, is demarked by the shelf break on the landward side; here the gradient changes from 1:1000, typical of the continental shelf, to steeper than 1:40. The continental slope may include a series of escarpments, or may itself be the landward side of a deep trench such as the Puerto Rican, Aleutian, or Peruvian trenches. The *continental rise*, at the foot of the continental slope, has gradients ranging from 1:1000 to 1:700. In many areas, it is a depositional feature. *Canyons*, such as the Hudson Canyon (Fig. 1–4), cut across the continental rise and act as channels for the seaward transport of sediment. Some canyons have continuations on the continental slopes and shelves, but many do not. In many parts of the world, the continental margin beyond the shelf consists of a deep trench and an outer ridge, as mentioned above. These trenches, especially prominent around the Pacific Ocean basin, are the deepest parts of the oceans, often exceeding six miles in depth.

The Ocean-Basin Floor

The ocean-basin floor includes everything seaward from the continental margin except for the major oceanic ridge systems. The floor makes up one-third of the Atlantic and Indian Ocean basins, and three-quarters of the Pacific

Topography and structure of ocean basins

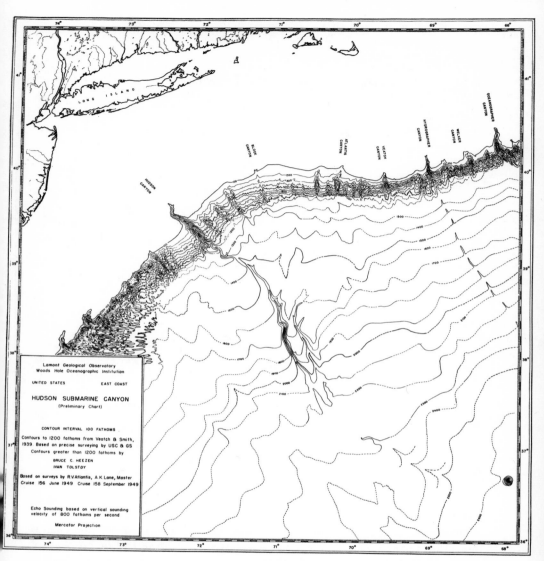

FIGURE 1–4 *Preliminary chart of Hudson Submarine Canyon, based on nonprecision soundings taken 1949–1950. (From Heezen, Tharp, and Ewing, 1959, by permission of The Geological Society of America.)*

Ocean basin. *Abyssal plains* adjacent to the continental rises—widespread in the Atlantic and sparse in the Pacific—are very smooth, with gradients between 1:1000 and 1:10,000. All abyssal plains are connected by canyons or other channels to landward sources of sediments, which are transported as dense slurries and deposited on the plains. Former abyssal plains that now exhibit rugged topography, apparently due to recent deformation, occur in the high central area of the Argentine basin and constitute major areas of the northeast Pacific ocean-basin floor. Most of the rest of the Pacific Ocean floor is occupied

Topography and structure of ocean basins

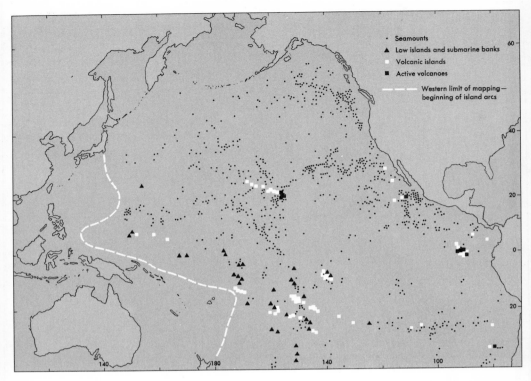

FIGURE 1-5 *The distribution of observed sea mounts, volcanic islands, and low islands (for example, atolls) and submarine banks in the Pacific Ocean. To date more than 2,000 such isolated features, with elevations of one kilometer or greater above the sea floor, have been discovered in all the oceans. There are probably at least ten times that number. (After Menard, 1964.)*

by abyssal hills forming a hummocky topography. These hills are probably caused by volcanic intrusions and extrusions. *Seamounts,* which do not penetrate the surface of the ocean, and *oceanic islands* such as the Hawaiian Islands are also of volcanic origin. Figure 1–5 shows the widespread occurrence of these volcanic features in the Pacific Ocean. In the Pacific Ocean the volcanic islands and seamounts commonly form clusters connected deep under the surface of the ocean by the accumulations from volcanic activity and the erosion of volcanoes. Topographically they look like featureless aprons around the volcanic peaks.

The Major Oceanic Ridge Systems

The major oceanic ridge systems form a series of connected, topographically high areas present in all the oceans (Fig. 1–6). Ridges are between 1,000 and 4,000 kilometers wide with a relief of two to four kilometers above the ocean floor, at points protruding from the sea surface as islands. The term "mid-oceanic ridge" has sometimes been used for the system, after the most prominent example, the mid-Atlantic ridge. The topography is representative of a composite of volcanic and rupture features called faults. At the center of the mid-Atlantic ridge, for example, there is a discontinuous "rift valley" characterized by heavy earthquake activity and higher-than-average heat flow. A series of transverse trenches that offset the axis of the ridge is also prominent. Other oceanic ridges, such as the East Pacific Rise, have many of the elements of the mid-Atlantic ridge but not necessarily all. Nevertheless, these differences aside, the ridges appear to be continuous around the Earth, except for offsetting by transverse breaks. They are a major feature of the ocean basins, coupled in some way to the location of continents.

Ocean-Bottom Structure

Having obtained a topographic picture of the ocean bottom, we can ask the next logical question: What are the physical properties and dimensions of the

FIGURE 1–6 *The major oceanic ridge systems. Because in the Atlantic Ocean the ridge system is almost exactly in the middle of the ocean the system is also called the "Mid-Oceanic" ridge system. The transverse faults are probably the result of differential movement of the ridge areas on either side of the faults due to ocean-floor spreading as described in Chapter 7. (After Heezen, 1963, in* The Sea, *ed. by Hill.)*

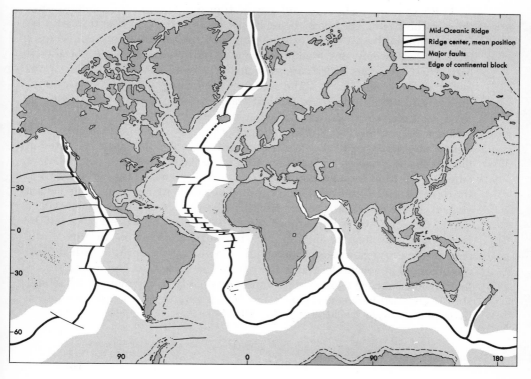

various types of rock and sediment that act as the "liners" of the ocean basin? In order to answer this question we must turn to the methods of geophysical exploration.

Seismic Refraction

The same principles that have been used to study the interior structure of the Earth by means of earthquakes can also be applied to the study of the structure of ocean basins. Earthquakes provide a large source of energy that is propagated as sound waves for great distances through the Earth's interior. The times of arrival of the different types of waves at various locations on the Earth, as measured by seismographs, can be used to determine the internal structure of the Earth. On a much smaller scale, man-made explosions can be used to generate sound waves that provide detailed information about the structure of the surface layers of the Earth, and it is this method that has been used successfully to determine the structure of ocean basins.

The technique of seismic refraction at sea makes use of sound waves supplied by an explosive set off from a ship. The sound waves penetrate the ocean bottom. The sediments and rocks of the ocean basins form a layered sequence in which each successively deeper layer has a higher velocity of propagation of sound waves than the one above. With such a configuration, the method of seismic refraction gives reasonable interpretations of the thickness and composition of each of the main layers.

As it was implied above, sound may be transmitted in several different ways through the Earth. The ocean, being liquid, can only support sound waves that are transmitted by a process of squeezing and release (compression and rarefaction), hence only this method of sound transmission need be considered here. These waves are called compressional waves and their velocities in various media are designated as V_p. (The subscript p refers to an early designation for the *primary* waves, which are the first waves, passing through the Earth's interior, that are recorded by a seismograph when an earthquake occurs.)

Since the various layers of the ocean bottom have different compressional-wave velocities, a particular sound ray from an explosion will be refracted at the interface of two layers into the plane of the layer it has just entered. As it moves away from the explosion source, it is continuously returned upward to the ocean surface until all its energy is dissipated. At any determined point away from the explosion, the first large signal on a recording instrument will be due to the sound traveling through the fastest path. The second pulse will be from sound traveling through the next fastest path and so on. In order to get enough data to define clearly the various major strata, records of arrival times are obtained at several locations away from the explosion. The waves are detected either aboard another ship whose distance from the moving "shooting" ship is changed between explosions or by a string of sound detectors, called hydrophones, towed behind the ship (Fig. 1-7).

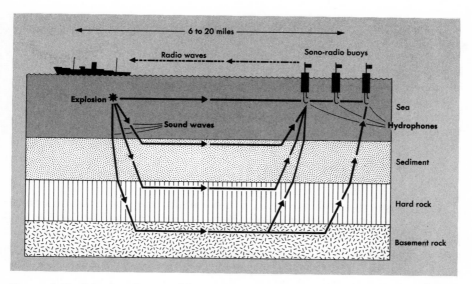

FIGURE 1-7 *Seismic refraction "shooting" using one ship and a string of towed sono-radio buoys. The relative dimensions of the ship and the various layers are exaggerated. Seismic refraction studies are also made with two ships, one shooting and the other receiving. The sound waves generated by the explosive are refracted at the boundaries of the different layers. For the sequence of materials normally encountered in the deep-sea layers, the velocity of sound increases progressively downward from layer to layer causing a return of the refracted signals at each interface. (After Hill, 1957.)*

The general structure of the deep ocean basins, as determined by using seismic refraction, is represented by the idealized layering of Table 1-1.

The Mohorovičić discontinuity noted in Table 1-1 marks the seismically determined interface between the crust of the Earth and the mantle. Measured

Table 1-1

Thickness and Properties
of the Layers of the Ocean Floor

Layer	Approximate Thickness (in Kilometers)	Velocity of Compressional Waves, V_p (Kilometers per second)	Likely Material	Approximate Density (in Grams per Cubic Centimeter)
Sea water	4.5	1.5	Sea water	1.0
Layer 1	0.45	2.0	Unconsolidated sediments	2.3
Layer 2—basement layer	1.75	4.0 to 6.0	Consolidated sediments or volcanic rocks	2.7
Layer 3—oceanic layer	4.7	6.7	Basalt (in part altered)	3.0
MOHOROVIČIĆ DISCONTINUITY				
Layer 4—mantle	—	8.1	Ultrabasic rocks	3.4

Topography and structure of ocean basins

from sea level, it occurs at an average depth of 40 kilometers under the continents and about 11 kilometers below the surface of the oceans. Since the Mohorovičić discontinuity (or the "Moho" as it is called) is only about six kilometers below the ocean floor, the first penetration through the crust into the mantle with a drill core will doubtless be done at sea. This proposed exploratory hole in the bottom of the sea has been called the "Mohole."

Gravity Measurements

Variations in the local distribution of mass in the layers of the Earth's crust and upper mantle affect instruments that are used to measure the Earth's gravity field. To a first approximation, the acceleration of gravity is constant over the Earth's surface. That is, a rock falling from a thousand-meter height any place in the world should have accelerated to the same velocity at the moment of impact with the ground. Similarly, a pendulum would have the same period all over the Earth if our approximation is valid, since the period is directly related to the acceleration of gravity. However, the period of a pendulum that is moved around the Earth, is greater at the equator than at higher latitudes. This fact was discovered when properly working pendulum clocks made in Europe were brought to the Caribbean and equatorial South America in the eighteenth and nineteenth centuries; they invariably ran slower than they did in the European homeland. This discrepancy could be explained by Newton's laws of gravity if either the mass of the Earth, as sensed by the pendulum were different in the two locations or if the distance to the center of mass were different. It was the latter alternative that best explained the tardy clocks. For at the equator the centrifugal force of the rotating Earth causes the Earth to be bulged out (and of course flattened at the poles). This bulging results in a greater distance to the center of the Earth (which corresponds well to the center of mass of the Earth), hence a lower acceleration due to gravity. Since the period of a pendulum is related to the acceleration of gravity, the result would be a slower-moving pendulum and a clock that always loses time at the equator if adjusted for the latitude of Paris or London (Fig. 1–8). The point is, then, that if we know the figure of the Earth, we can predict the acceleration of gravity to expect at any latitude.

The modern-day geophysicist uses a similar pendulum mechanism to measure the variation in the acceleration of gravity over the Earth's surface. A gravimeter, as the pendulum and other instruments for measuring gravity are called when used as a geophysicist's instrument, records the effects of local excess or deficiency of mass in modifying the acceleration of gravity that is predicted for a given latitude from the Earth's figure. Until the 1960's the only stable platform at sea on which a gravimeter could be operated and give significant results was aboard submarines below the action of the ocean waves. But now, with proper instrument platforms, gravimeters can easily be used on surface ships.

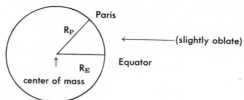

R_P = Distance from center of mass to the surface at Paris

R_E = Distance from center of mass to the surface at Equator

	AT PARIS	AT EQUATOR
Gravitational acceleration (g) (G = universal gravitational constant; m = mass of pendulum; M = mass of Earth)	$$g_P = \frac{GmM}{R_P{}^2}$$	$$g_E = \frac{GmM}{R_E{}^2}$$
Period (T) of pendulum with length l	$$T_P = \pi\sqrt{\frac{l}{g_P}}$$	$$T_E = \pi\sqrt{\frac{l}{g_E}}$$
Period is proportional to distance from center of Earth	$$T_P = R_P\left(\frac{\pi^2 l}{GmM}\right)^{\!\frac{1}{2}}$$	$$T_E = R_E\left(\frac{\pi^2 l}{GmM}\right)^{\!\frac{1}{2}}$$

Hence if R_E is greater than R_P (as it is) then T_E is greater than T_P and a pendulum clock will run slower at the Equator when set correctly for the latitude of Paris.

FIGURE 1–8 *The period of a pendulum is controlled by the gravitational accelerations. A pendulum clock set precisely at the latitude of Paris was found to run more slowly when transported to the equator. This effect is explained by the oblateness of the Earth because of its rotation.*

Gravity measurements at sea show differences due to local variations in mass distribution resulting from the varying thicknesses of the layers of the oceanic crust and upper mantle. The gravity results are best used in conjunction with seismic data and with the measured or inferred density of the various layers that have been determined seismically. Along the continental margins, for example, the location of the Mohorovičić discontinuity is not clearly delineated by seismic data. Although the discovery of this major world-wide discontinuity was made on the basis of seismic refraction studies, we know that it is also a discontinuity between material of different densities as seen in Table 1–1. The depth of the Mohorovičić discontinuity thus may be inferred from gravity data, by assigning densities to the major rock or sediment layers and determining the thickness of each layer that would be compatible with the local gravity measurements (Fig. 1–9).

Through the use of gravity and seismic data, the faulted nature of many of the deep-sea trenches at the margins of the ocean basins has been shown; specifically, gravity measurements above trenches show deficiencies of mass

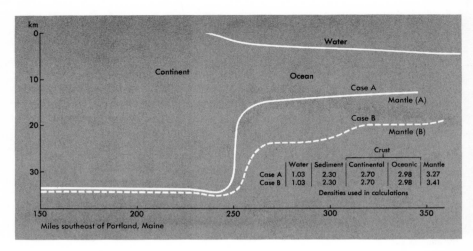

FIGURE 1–9 *Using gravity measurements it is possible to determine the location of the crust-mantle boundary under the continental margin where seismic refraction cannot be used. Case A is preferred to Case B because it is more compatible with the seismically determined crust-mantle depth under the oceans. The densities for all layers but the mantle are based on materials that are observed and have acceptable seismic velocities as well. (After Drake, Ewing, and Sutton, 1959.)*

compared to the adjacent ocean-basin floor. The origin of the trenches is not known; we do know, though, that the margins of the oceans are under great stress and that buckling and faulting might be expected there. Figure 1–10 shows a representative structural section across a trench based on seismic and gravity data.

FIGURE 1–10 *Computed crustal section across the Puerto Rico trench (on the north side of Puerto Rico). The crustal layering is based on seismic data and the crust-mantle boundary (equivalent to the Mohorovičić seismic discontinuity) is based on gravity measurements. Where the gravity and seismic crust-mantle boundaries can be compared, they are fairly close. The measured velocity of primary waves (V_P) are related to rock types and their inferred densities (After Talwani, Sutton, and Worzel, 1959.)*

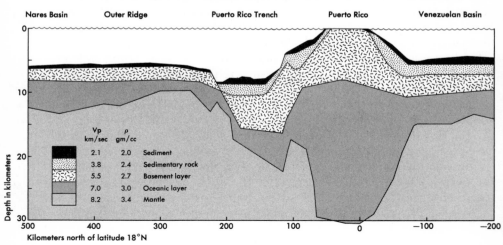

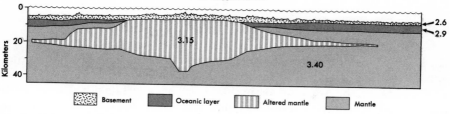

Basement   Oceanic layer   Altered mantle   Mantle

FIGURE 1–11 *A possible crustal model across the north Mid-Atlantic Ridge that satisfies both the gravity data and the seismic data. The inferred densities used in the model are given on the figure for each unit. The 3.15 density rock underlying the ridge area is the "anomalous" mantle, referred to in the text, having a seismic primary wave velocity of 7.3 kilometers per second compared to the normal mantle velocity of 8.1 kilometers per second. The sediment and sedimentary rock layers are too thin along the ridge to appear in the diagram. (After Talwani, LePichon, and Ewing, 1965.)*

Crustal structures of the oceanic ridge systems are also inferred from both seismic and gravity data. For instance, the seismic data indicate that, in addition to the layers in the "normal" section described in Table 1–1, underneath the axis of the ridge a layer with a velocity of about 7.3 kilometers per second is encountered in the mantle. Normal mantle velocity under both continents and oceans is about 8.1 kms./second. The low velocity of the mantle layer under the ridge is due to less dense material (possibly a rock like serpentine formed by the hydration of ultrabasic rocks of the mantle). The gravity data give dimensions of the various velocity layers when an appropriate density, based on the inferred rock type, is assigned to each layer. These results on a section across a typical part of the major ocean ridge system are shown in Fig. 1–11.

Seismic Reflection—
The Structures and Thicknesses of the Sediment Layers

Seismic refraction data, although useful for delineating the major units of the deep-sea floor, give very little information on the sedimentary layer ("Layer 1") itself. Seismic reflection, however, is more sensitive to the presence of differences in sedimentary layering that result in distinct reflection horizons for sound waves. The techniques are similar to the method of seismic refraction except that generally smaller energy sources are required and sound detectors must be close to the ship emitting the signal in order to record the waves bouncing from acoustic reflectors in the sediments.

It had been observed before 1961 that, in both seismic refraction work and continuous echo sounding, reflection horizons in sediments could be detected. By this method a continuous layer of volcanic ash was discovered in the East Pacific, for instance. Since 1961 the technique of using *seismic reflection* at sea has been perfected for investigating sedimentary structure and thickness. The energy pulses are supplied by explosive charges (for deep penetration into the sediment), by electric spark "pingers" (similar to the equipment used in obtaining echo soundings but at different frequencies so as to diminish attenuation by sound absorption by the sediments), and more recently by compressed air. Equipped with these devices, oceanographers have explored the structure and thickness of sediments of the major oceanic areas.

For instance, the Argentine Basin (Fig. 1–12) has a section of sediment 3,000 meters thick, one of the thickest accumulations in the deep sea. The sediments smooth out a rough topography of basement rock, possibly basalt of volcanic origin. A particularly strong reflecting horizon ("Horizon A"), seen at a depth of 500 meters or more below the ocean floor, indicates a major change in the constitution of the sediment. Maurice Ewing, who has studied this area intensively with his colleagues at the Lamont Geological Observatory, has suggested that the horizon may represent a fossil abyssal plain with strongly stratified deposits carried to the deep ocean bottom by strong bottom currents. Horizon A seems to be present in other parts of the oceans as well. If these instances are all truly contemporaneous then an event of ocean-wide significance has been recorded.

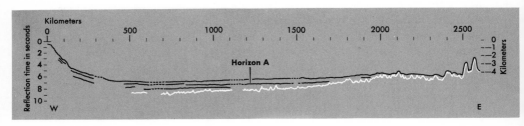

FIGURE 1–12   *Seismic reflection section across the Argentine Basin from the Continental slope off northern Argentina to the flank of the mid-Atlantic ridge. Horizon A is a strong reflecting layer that may be traced for great distances. (After Ewing, Ludwig, and Ewing, 1964.)*

FIGURE 1–13   *Seismic reflection section across the mid-Atlantic ridge in a line between Dakar, Senegal, and Halifax, Canada (Nova Scotia). The black areas represent the sediments, showing "ponding." The sediments on the ridges follow the topography as a thin veneer (50 meters or less). In many places photographs show little or no sediment on volcanic rock. (After Ewing, Ewing and Talwani, 1964.)*

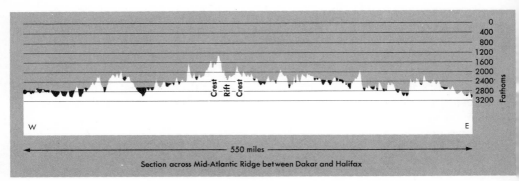

Section across Mid-Atlantic Ridge between Dakar and Halifax

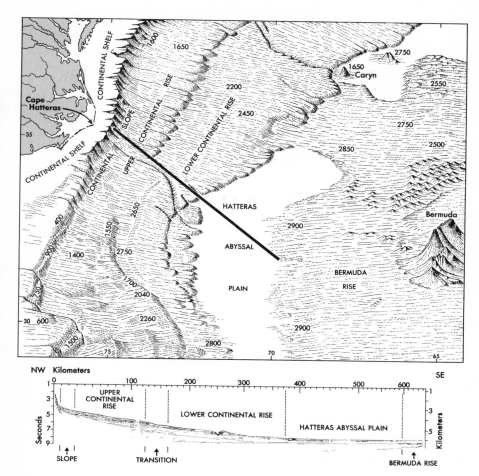

FIGURE 1-14 *A line drawing from a continuous seismic reflection profile between the continental slope off Cape Hatteras, North Carolina, and the Bermuda Rise. Distance along the profile, direction, and physiographic provinces are marked at the top of the profile. Two-way travel time of the acoustic pulse (from source near surface—to reflector— to receiver near surface) is indicated at the left margin. Depth below sea level in kilometers is indicated at the right margin. The configuration of the bottom and of reflectors beneath the bottom is distinctive under each physiographic province. Numbers on chart are fathoms. (After Rona and Clay, 1967.)*

In contrast to the Argentine Basin the sediments along the mid-Atlantic Ridge are not thick (Fig. 1–13), averaging 50 meters. Since the thickness of sediments is barely measurable in many parts, it appears that the sediment layer follows the rugged topography of the ridge except in places where layers have been slumped away or where intermontane "ponding" has occurred.

The sedimentary structure of the continental margin (Fig. 1–14) reflects the processes of erosion and deposition occurring there. The thicknesses here are the greatest of all, since the margins are the major traps for sediments from the continents.

2

Sediments

and their transport

Speaking in the broadest possible terms, the beginning point of the oceanic deposition of sediments begins on land and runs as follows: Rocks exposed above sea level become subject to chemical action, especially chemical influences associated with life; this process is called *weathering*. Some elements, leached from the rocks by weathering, are carried to the sea in solution; much of the remaining altered rock material becomes a complex of degradation products, such as clay and sand, characteristic of the local climate and general environment. These products of weathering are carried, by streams primarily, to the sea, together with particles from easily eroded rocks which may not be strongly altered chemically. Material may also be supplied to the ocean basins by mechanisms other than streams that drain the continents. The products of oceanic volcanoes or of continental glaciers are also found on the ocean floor. In this chapter, we discuss the composition of sediments and the transport of particles both to and within the oceans.

The Composition of Sediments

Marine sediments are composed of detrital material from land and substances extracted from solution by biological or chemical processes. There are two gross classifications we can apply to marine sediments without being concerned about how a particular sediment got where it did. One is based on the grain size of the sediment (Table 2–1), the other on its composition (Fig. 2–1).

If a sediment on the ocean floor contains particles nearly all of one size range, the sediment is *well-sorted*. Similarly, a sediment

FIGURE 2–1 *The range of sedimentary rock types represented as mixtures of three components: calcium (plus magnesium) carbonates, clay minerals (represented by the hypothetical hydrated aluminum and iron oxides as the end member), and silicia (silicon dioxide). Sediments and sedimentary rocks have the same ranges of composition. Iron-rich laterites and aluminum-rich bauxites are the products of intense weathering. Sandstones are primarily composed of indurated sandy sediments, in many cases dominantly quartz. Cherts are the sedimentary rock equivalent of biologically deposited siliceous deposits. During the transformation into rock the amorphous silica, originally deposited by diatoms and radiolarians, is transformed into a very hard microcrystalline quartz-rich rock. Argillaceous (from French argile, for clay) rocks are derived from the lithification of clay-rich muds. Sediments or sedimentary rocks rarely, if ever, have compositions represented by the unpatterned area of the triangle. (After Mason, 1967.)*

Table 2–1

Sizes of Sedimentary Components*

Name	Particle Diameter (in Millimeters)
Boulders	Greater than 256
Cobbles	64 to 256
Pebbles	4 to 64
Granules	2 to 4
Sand	0.062 to 2
Silt	0.004 to 0.062
Clay	Less than 0.004

* Commonly called the "Wentworth scale."

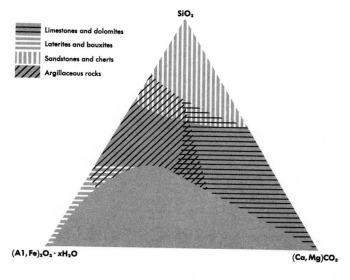

Limestones and dolomites
Laterites and bauxites
Sandstones and cherts
Argillaceous rocks

SiO_2

$(Al, Fe)_2O_3 \cdot xH_2O$

$(Ca, Mg)CO_3$

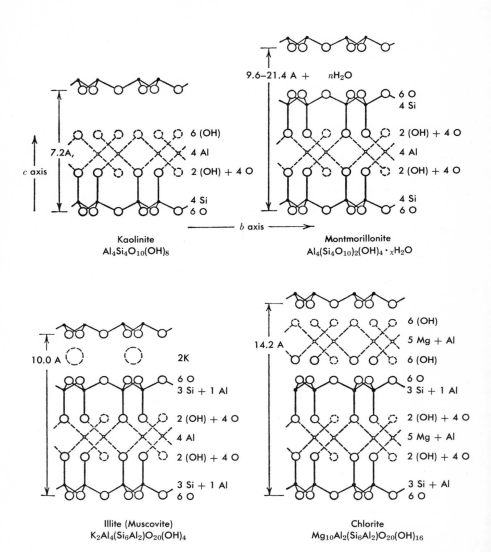

FIGURE 2–2 *Diagrams looking at right angles to the sheets making up the main structure of the clay minerals. The silica and associated layers are stacked along the c-axis. The kaolinite sheets are held together by weak hydrogen bonds. Montmorillonite as shown is representative of a group of similar minerals in which substitutions of iron and magnesium occur at various sites. The iron-rich montmorillonite is the dominant mineral of deep-sea clays of the South Pacific. They share the property of holding water molecules between the sheets, causing expansion and contraction along the c-axis during hydration and dessication repectively. The montmorillonite minerals also show a high capacity to exchange cations. Illite is the term used for the sedimentary fine-grained equivalent of ordinary mica (muscovite). The chlorite crystal represented here can be modified into an iron-rich form. Deep-sea sediments commonly contain this more iron-rich form. (After Mason, 1967.)*

composed of one mineralogical or chemical type is *very pure*. Most sediments, however, are neither perfectly well-sorted nor very pure; but it is precisely the information contained in the mixtures that is of great value in determining the history of the sediment. Of particular interest, because of their extensive distributions are the clay- and sand-size components. The mineralogical composition in these size ranges varies considerably, depending on the sources of material.

Clay-size Fraction

Although the clay-size fraction (or portion of sediments) may contain fine-grained calcium carbonate, it is composed mainly of silicate and oxide minerals. The most important of these are the *clay minerals*, which are the silicate minerals formed from normal rocks either by weathering or the action of hot water from volcanic and other thermal sources. The principle clay minerals are kaolinite, montmorillonite, illite (or mica), and chlorite. The clay minerals, structurally, are related to the common mineral mica in that sheets, formed by the joining together of silica tetrahedra in a two-dimensional array, constitute the basic structural units (Fig. 2–2). The deviations from the mica structure and the variations among clay minerals are due to the way the silica sheets are stacked with other chemical layers and the degree of chemical substitution within both the original silica sheet and the added layers. Most of the clay minerals found in sediments are derived from weathering profiles on the continents and alteration products of volcanic rocks. They may be modified to some degree by interactions with sea water.

Sand- and Silt-size Fractions

The next coarser fraction of sediments ranges from the calcium carbonate debris of shells to a variety of silicate and oxide minerals.

Most of the carbonate minerals deposited in the oceans are due to the action of organisms. Calcium carbonate in one of three forms is the primary deposit: *Aragonite* is laid down by most present-day corals and some molluscs (Fig. 2–3); *low-magnesium calcite* is deposited by some molluscs, some foraminifera (including all the deep-sea species), brachiopods, and the unicellular plant family *Coccolithophoridae* (a major constituent of deep-sea sediments and the main component of the chalks of the White Cliffs of Dover) (Fig. 2–4); and *high-magnesium calcite* is derived from echinoderms and some large foraminifera in shallow waters (Fig. 2–5). Only the molluscs commonly have species whose shells (or *tests*) are layers of aragonite and low-magnesium calcite.

In the geologic record, the older the rocks the less well preserved aragonite is, because it is not the stable state of calcium carbonate at low pressures. It is commonly replaced by calcite, even in some relatively young coral reefs now exposed above sea level, as in the Florida Keys.

Sediments and their transport

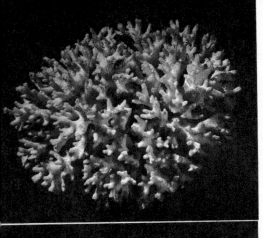

FIGURE 2–3 *Aragonite-depositing marine organisms. (Top) Coral. All common reef-building corals deposit pure aragonite shells. This is the common "lace coral" (diameter about 8"). (Bottom) Mollusc. Both snails and clams have species that deposit aragonite in various amounts. This marine snail, Conus-gloria maris (about 2" long), deposits a pure aragonitic shell, as does the chambered nautilus, a representative of another type of mollusc, related to the octopus and the squid. (Both courtesy American Museum of Natural History.)*

FIGURE 2–4 *Low-magnesium calcite-depositing marine organisms. (A) Mollusc. This is the common oyster which deposits a pure low-magnesium calcite shell. (Courtesy Carolina Biological Supply Company.) (B) Pelagic foraminiferan. This test (Globigerina bulloides), is from the Scotian Shelf. Magnification 195x. (Courtesy G. A. Bartlett, Bedford Institute of Oceanography.) (C) Coccolithophore. This is a shell deposited by a common type of marine plant (phytoplankton). The species is Coccolithus huxleyi. This coccosphere disaggregates during deposition and is rarely preserved intact. The component "ovals" and smaller platelets are common components of deep-sea sediments and many chalk deposits like the White Cliffs of Dover. Magnification 10,350x. (Courtesy, A. McIntyre, Lamont Geological Observatory.)*

A

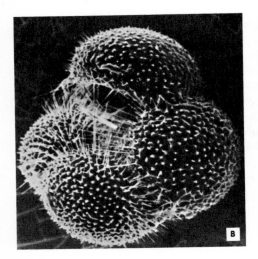

B

C

Dolomite, a carbonate mineral having equal numbers of calcium and magnesium atoms in its crystal lattice, is not a primary deposit. It occurs commonly in the geologic record, however, and for this reason has aroused a great deal of investigation and speculation regarding its origin. Recently it has been discovered that in part, it is the probable reaction product of brines, formed by evaporation, with aragonite crystals deposited by organisms. This origin is compatible with many occurrences in the geologic record.

FIGURE 2-5 *High-magnesium calcite-depositing marine organism. The echinoderms are echinoids (sea urchins), crinoids, and starfishes. This is* Centrechinus antillarum, *a tropical Atlantic species of purple sea urchin (diameter about 6"). High-magnesium calcite shells can contain up to 15% magnesium. (Courtesy Carolina Biological Supply Company.)*

The sand fraction of sediments, aside from the calcium carbonate component, is composed of minerals generally resistant to weathering. The most common of these is quartz. In certain parts of the world other minerals, more resistant and more dense than quartz, are also concentrated as sands. If the concentration is sufficiently great and the minerals are of economic interest a fortune can be found on the seashore—for instance, the tin-bearing cassiterite sands and nearby ruby-bearing sands of Malaya, the diamond-bearing sands of southwest Africa, and the sands of South Carolina rich in rare-earth minerals.

Other "heavy minerals," less spectacular than those cited above, are also found in the coarse-grained fraction and have been useful in determining sources of sediments and paths of transport.

Particles in Fluids

Dust storms and muddy rivers are ample proof that fluids can transport particles. In this section we will review the general laws that govern the transport and deposition of particles in fluids in order to understand the laws that control marine sedimentation.

Stokes' Law

A fundamental consequence of Newton's laws of motion is that, regardless of mass or dimensions, *in a vacuum* all bodies have the same acceleration at the surface of the Earth. It is also a fundamental observation of parachutists that free fall does not result in the continuously increasing velocity predicted by a constant acceleration, but that a constant *terminal velocity* is reached, at which point air drag prevents further increase in velocity and acceleration becomes zero. This terminal velocity is a function of the density and shape of the body and the density of air, which varies with temperature and height.

The fall of very small sand- and clay-size particles through air and water is controlled by the same law, and for such small sizes this rule is formalized as *Stokes' Law:* For spherical particles of varying size but of the same density falling through a fluid, the fall velocity of each particle is proportional to the square of its radius (see Table 2–2). Hence, larger particles will settle out of a given column of water or air faster than smaller particles. Corrections must be made, though, if the particles have a variety of shapes, since the drag will be greater for flat, platy particles than for spherical ones. Also, in water, mineral particles having a diameter greater than 25 microns obey more complicated laws as a result of increased resistance of the fluid to the particles due to impact with the water as they descend.

Motion in Fluids

There are two main types of motion in fluids: laminar flow and turbulent flow. *Laminar* flow, as the name implies, involves the coherent movement of water molecules in stream lines. Particles suspended in the fluid move with the velocity of the laminar layers while also settling out under the force of gravity

Table 2–2

Stokes' Law of Settling Velocities

$$\text{Stokes' Law: } v = \frac{D^2 \rho_p - \rho_f g}{18\eta}$$

v = velocity of fall (cm/sec)
D = diameter (cm)
ρ_p = density of particle (g/cm^3)

ρ_f = density of fluid (g/cm^3)
g = acceleration of gravity (cm/sec^2) = 980 cm/sec^2
η = viscosity (poise = g/sec cm)

For spheres of quartz (ρ_p = 2.6 g/cm^3) falling through ocean water (ρ_f = 1.0 g/cm^3) at a temperature of 10°C (η = 0.0140 poise). Stokes' Law holds for particles up to 100 microns radius (200 microns diameter). Above that size a modification (Oseen's equation) is used to account for nonlaminar behavior of the fluid due to impact by the particle.

Radius in Microns ($\mu = 10^{-4}$ cm)	Velocity (cm/sec)	Time To Fall through 4,000 Meters
1	0.00025	51 years
10	0.025	185 days
100 (Stokes')	2.5	1.8 days
100 (modified Oseen's)	1.7	2.7 days

according to Stokes' Law. In *turbulent* flow the molecules of the fluid and the associated particles do not move along stream lines. Since there is turbulence in large fluid bodies like the oceans and the atmosphere, what then is the role of turbulence in sediment transport? Turbulence of itself does not keep particles in suspension more efficiently than a fluid with either laminar or negligible motion, *if* a continuous source of particles is not available. If, however, a source of particles remains available, then the net effect is to approach a steady state of quantity and size distribution in the fluid; this state will be characteristic of the rate of movement of the fluid. Empirical relationships between the fate of various sizes of particles and the velocity of flowing water have been observed (Fig. 2–6). As can be seen in the Figure very fine particles, for instance, will be moved at even low velocities.

Now that we have considered what sediments are composed of and the general behavior of particles in fluids, we can turn to the problem of how sediments get to the oceans.

FIGURE 2–6 *Estimated current velocities for erosion, transportation, and sedimentation of different-sized particles (diameter in millimeters). Cohesive materials are typically muds composed of clay minerals and organic-rich sediments. 100 centimeters/second = 3.6 kilometers/hour = about 2 miles/hour. (After Heezen and Hollister, 1964.)*

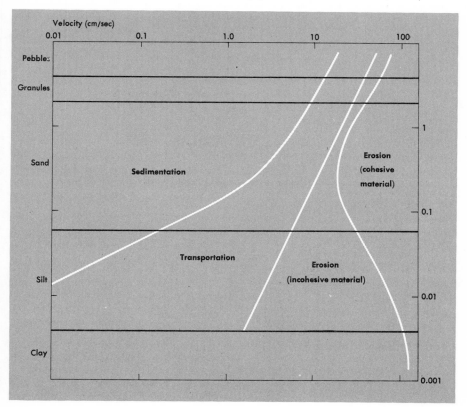

Transport of Particles to the Oceans

The major sources of sediments to the oceans are the atmosphere, glaciers, and streams. The last of these is by far the most important, but it is obvious that the contributions from the other sources, where recognizable, provide valuable information on climate and wind patterns.

Atmospheric Transport

As with flowing water, an air mass moving across land will develop, as a function of velocity, a steady-state concentration of suspended material of various sizes. Once the air mass is over water, the particles should be expected to fall out in the ocean, following Stokes' Law. Figure 2–7 shows the observed dust-storm patterns observed at sea and in particular shows the strong extension from the Sahara desert over the Atlantic Ocean. Actually, at the ocean surface, entrapment by waves and spray accelerates the removal of particles during the downward motion of their turbulent paths; the result is a more rapid removal of particles from the air mass than is predicted by Stokes' Law.

Particles smaller than about 15 microns (0.015 millimeters) will remain aloft so long, according to the settling velocity predicted by Stokes' Law, that the main mechanism of removal from the atmosphere is entrapment in rain and snow. That is why radioactive fallout injected into the lower portion of the atmosphere, called the troposphere, is removed, for any latitude, more efficiently in areas of high precipitation and less efficiently over deserts.

If particles are injected into the stratosphere (above about 60,000 feet), as in violent volcanic explosions such as Krakatoa in 1882 or in the detonation of highly energetic nuclear devices, they must settle through the stratosphere without the help of precipitation. Hence, these particles are distributed worldwide. Once in the troposphere, however, they are most effectively transported to the Earth's surface by precipitation.

Glacial Transport

Continental glaciers, as in Antarctica and Greenland, are efficient agents of erosion and sediment transport. Where glaciers end on land, their sediments become part of the general supply of debris to streams and thus may be diluted to the point that they cannot be distinguished in marine deposits. But when the glaciers end at the edge of the sea, as in Antarctica and Greenland, the debris is deposited directly on the sea floor. If meltwaters are the main form of terminal transport, deposition in fjords and deltas is common, and the fate of the particles is similar to that of those supplied by streams. Grains of sand,

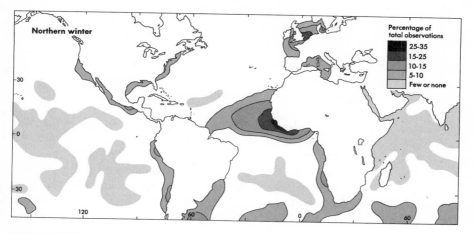

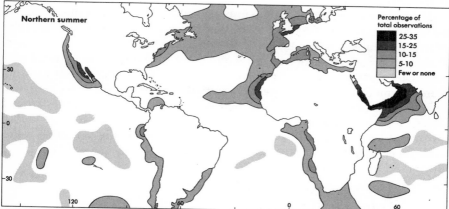

FIGURE 2–7   *Frequency of haze over the ocean produced by wind-borne dust from the continents. There is evidence that some dust from Africa travels as far west as Barbados. (After Arrhenius, 1963, in* The Sea *ed. by Hill.)*

however, will show pressure-induced marks acquired during abrasion by the glacier, thus distinguishing them from purely stream-borne sediments.

Where the ends of the glaciers break off into the sea (a process called *calving*), icebergs are formed; since these may move far out to sea before melting completely, deposits of coarse material can occur in the deep ocean. Such glacial marine deposits fringe Antarctica and Greenland, and boulders have been found in deep-sea sediments as far as icebergs drift toward lower latitudes.

Stream Transport

The rivers of the world denude continents of weathered material to the greatest extent of all. The quantity of suspended load carried by the major rivers of the world has been estimated to be about 30×10^{15} grams per year.

This figure corresponds to a concentration of suspended sediment, on the average, of 0.5 grams per liter. The traction load at the bottom of streams ("bed load") is more difficult to estimate, but is probably no more than 10 per cent of the suspended load.

There are four major modes of deposition of the suspended load of the river once it reaches the oceans. The sediments are deposited: (1) on the broad, virtually featureless continental shelf, primarily in bays and inlets, such as Chesapeake Bay or Long Island Sound; (2) in offshore basins, as off southern California; (3) in deltas, such as those of the Mississippi, Rhine, and Nile; or (4) in abyssal plains directly, as with the Congo and Magdalena (in Colombia) Rivers, bypassing the narrow continental shelf along a continuous submarine canyon to the abyssal plain.

Most of these sediments end up in bays, deltas, or offshore basins, which all act as settling basins. The velocity of the stream is terminated, and from the relatively calm sea water the particles settle out according to Stokes' Law. Hence, the coarsest particles are found closest to shore. Some of the finest-sized clay particles may be retained in tidal marshes by the grasses growing there but much of the fine material is carried out further by surface currents, to be dropped on the deep ocean bottom. Direct deposition on the abyssal plains, by way of submarine canyons, is not as common now as it was during the glacial ages, when sea level was lowered 300 feet by the storage of water as ice on continents.

Transport of Particles within the Oceans

Once particles are brought to the oceans they may be redistributed by a variety of forces acting in the oceans. These may strongly modify the initial distribution patterns controlled by the source of supply from the continents.

Surface Currents

The prevailing winds acting on the ocean surface set up the major surface-current patterns. These are shown for the Atlantic Ocean in Fig. 2–8, the most prominent feature in the North Atlantic being the Gulf Stream. The surface currents move with velocities as great as three knots (that is, nautical miles per hour), so that complete circulation of the surface water is accomplished in a few years. The fine-grained particles are carried with these currents, and with their long settling times, they have a more generalized distribution than coarser-grained particles.

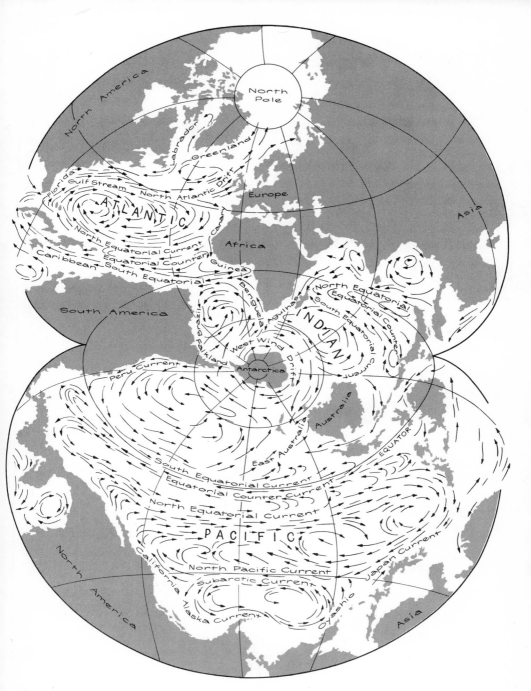

FIGURE 2–8 *The surface currents of the oceans. The pattern of gyres (clockwise in the northern hemisphere and counterclockwise in the southern hemisphere) can be explained as the result of the major global wind patterns—the prevailing westerlies blowing from west to east at about 40°N and 40°S and the trade winds blowing from east to west just north and south of the equator. (From "The Circulation of the Oceans" by Walter Munk.*
Copyright © 1955 by Scientific American, Inc. All rights reserved.)

Sediments and their transport

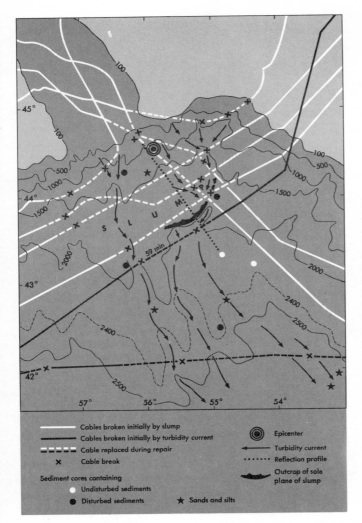

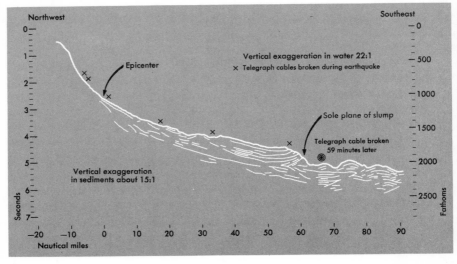

FIGURE 2–9 *The Grand Banks slump of 1929. In 1929 an earthquake on the Grand Banks near the Laurentian Channel resulted in the breakage of a number of transoceanic cables. All cables within 60 miles south of the epicenter of the earthquake broke instantly. Later, a series of breaks occurred as the result of a slump and related turbidity currents. The turbidity currents seem to have moved down three separate channels. (Top) A map of the cables and the lines of movement. (Bottom) A profile along the dotted line on the map. shows the disturbed sediments and the "sole" plane of slumping sediment along which movement occurred. (After Heezen and Drake, 1964.)*

Turbidity Currents

The transport of sediment downslope, primarily along submarine canyons, occurs when a sediment slurry moves as a coherent fluid with a density greater than that of sea water. Such a fluid in motion is called a turbidity current. A slide or slump of sediment somewhere on the continental margin initiates the action. The triggering mechanism of downslope movement may be an earthquake, a hurricane hitting near shore, or high-sediment discharge by streams, either bed load or settled suspended load; after a long period of deposition this deposit would begin downslope slumping.

The movements of turbidity currents resulting from earthquakes have consequences of concern to man. For instance, the Grand Banks earthquake of 1929 resulted in downslope movement of sediment that sequentially broke the transatlantic cables in that region. Figure 2–9 shows an analysis of this event.

Turbidity currents undoubtedly are the main mechanism of transport of material to the abyssal plains, as is indicated by layers of silt and sand and by the presence of plant remains from nearshore environments that were swept out by the currents. When the turbidity current has run its course, the debris it is carrying settles out from still water, resulting in graded bedding due to the varied settling rates of fine and coarse particles, as predicted by Stokes' Law.

Bottom Currents

Oceanographic observations of various kinds indicate the presence of currents on the bottom of some parts of the ocean that are strong enough to move sediments. They are four main types of evidence: (1) In order to maintain the balance of water moving in the Atlantic Ocean basin, strong northward-moving bottom currents must be postulated for the western South Atlantic to balance the shallower southward transport. (2) Floats that can maintain their location at a designated depth in the ocean show strong currents even at great depths, and current meters have been used actually to measure currents at the bottom. These indicate velocities up to several knots. (3) Photographs of the bottom show features that can be attributed only to strong currents. These are ripple marks, scour marks, linear features formed in the direction of current movements, bare rock, and coarse residues (Fig. 2–10). (4) By standard oceanographic techniques described in Chapter 4, cores of the sediments on the ocean floor are raised; some of these show strong cross-stratification, indicating the action of currents.

"Deep-Water" Transport

It is possible to determine the concentration of fine particles in sea water by observing the scattering of light, or by actually recovering the material by

FIGURE 2–10 *Ripple marks with wave lengths of a foot or so in two directions indicating deep currents with variable directions. Foraminiferan tests are found in the troughs of the ripples. This photograph was taken at 2,333 fathoms (4,250 meters) in the Drake Passage (57°28′S 64°51′W) southeast of Cape Horn. (Courtesy H. Grant Goodell, Florida State University.)*

passing the water through filters with small pores, or by centrifuging it. Studies have been made of various marine environments by all these methods. Fine material from the Po River, for instance, has been traced as a deep layer in the Adriatic Sea. Recently, by means of a photographic measurement device for scattered light, a cloudy, or "nepheloid," layer has been observed, one that appears to be continuous and conforms roughly to the bottom topography at least in the northwest Atlantic. This layer indicates the possible deep-water transport of clay-size material to the abyssal plain from the continental margin by means other than turbidity currents, the particulars of which are as yet unknown.

3

Deep-sea sediments

The sand-size fraction of stream sediments, as well as some of the finer material, is largely deposited in nearshore areas. About 10 per cent of the stream-borne sediments, however, ultimately end up on the deep ocean floor. Along with these sediments, the windblown, volcanic, and glacially derived components plus biogenic calcium carbonate and silica add up to a variety of deposits of considerable geologic interest on the deep ocean floor. The proper interpretation of these deposits tells us a great deal about Earth history: climatic variations, patterns of ancient oceanic and wind currents, the denudation of the continents, and structural history.

Since other volumes in this series are concerned with the record in nearshore sediments,* our primary interest in this chapter will be the deep-sea sediments, that is, those found in all parts of the ocean except the continental shelf, regardless of their mode of origin.

The first detailed study of the sediments at the bottom of the deep ocean was made at the end of the nineteenth century

---

* See A. L. Bloom, *The Surface of the Earth*, L. F. Laporte, *Ancient Environments*, and D. L. Eicher, *Geologic Time*.

by Sir John Murray and A. F. Renard. Using samples that had been obtained from all the world oceans by the voyage of H. M. S. *Challenger* in the early 1870's, they classified the deep-sea sediments in terms of the dominant components obvious to the unaided eye. Hence the terms "red clay," "globigerina ooze," and "siliceous ooze" were coined. These terms remain valuable for the most general descriptions, although we have now become aware of the complexity of the mineralogy of deep-sea sediments. For instance, the term "red clay," as originally used, not only subsumed a wide range of clay minerals but was also applied to sediments primarily composed of other nonclay silicate minerals. "Globigerina ooze" included almost all sediments rich in calcium carbonate that were composed of coccoliths and the tests of foraminifera. Siliceous oozes were generally of two types, those rich in radiolarian tests and those rich in diatom tests.

In classifying deep-sea sediments today, we can take advantage of the large amount of detailed work done in the last 50 years on both the identification and the origins of the components. Table 3–1 presents a classification of the components of deep-sea deposits on the basis of their source and method of transport. From such a list a particular sample can be described in terms of the dominant components.

A more detailed discussion of each of the major components and its distribution on the sea floor is the substance of this chapter.

Table 3–1

Classification of Deep-sea Components

1. *Pelagic biogenic:* The remains of organisms: calcareous and siliceous tests and organic and phosphatic material.
2. *Nonbiogenic:* The sedimentary components not originating from life processes in the ocean.
   a. *Pelagic detrital:* This term is restricted to nonbiogenic components originating near the surface of the ocean and deposited on the sea floor by settling.
   b. *Bottom-transported detrital:* This material, typically transported by turbidity and bottom currents, contains silts and sands and remains of shallow-water organisms and land materials. There is also a fine-grained component that, at the seaward side of abyssal plains, may not be easily distinguishable from the pelagic detrital component.
   c. *Indigenous deposits:* These are derived within the ocean basin itself by a variety of processes, such as submarine reaction of volcanic material with sea water, migration and reconstitution of materials in the sediments, and weathering of volcanic materials exposed above sea level.

Biogenic Components

A wide variety of marine organisms deposit, besides organic compounds, hard parts that serve for structural support or protection. The common deposits that persist long enough to become components in sediments are calcium carbonate, silicon dioxide (or "silica"), calcium phosphate in the form of the mineral apatite (typical of bones and teeth), and some organic compounds. There are some unusual compounds that organisms are known to deposit, but they are rarely, if ever, preserved in identifiable form in sediments. One group of radiolarian, for instance, deposits a test made exclusively of strontium sulfate (the mineral celestite) and certain molluscs (the chitons) have hard rasping organs made of an oxide of iron. In the following section we shall discuss the major biogenic components of deep-sea sediments.

Calcium Carbonate

Foraminiferan tests, coccoliths, and pteropod tests are the principle constituents of the calcium carbonate ($CaCO_3$) in deep-sea sediments. The foraminiferan shells found in deep-sea sediments are all composed of calcite. Coccoliths, the calcite tests of the algal family Coccolithophoridae, account for most of the fine-grained (less than 30 microns in diameter) carbonate material in deep-sea sediments. Pteropods are molluscs with aragonitic shells (Fig. 3–1). Their remains are preserved in deep-sea sediments at water depths of less than 3,500 meters. The term "globigerina ooze" applies to deep-sea sediments that are rich in a mixture of foraminiferan tests and coccoliths. A wide range of species of each group are found.

The calcium carbonate concentration of deep-sea sediments is a direct reflection of the relative rates of accumulation of clay and calcium carbonate. The regional distribution of calcium carbonate concentration in deep-sea sediments shows three major features, as seen in the Atlantic Ocean (Fig. 3–2): (1) The topographic high points have sediments that are generally rich in $CaCO_3$. (2) In some, but not all, areas where the ocean surface is organically very productive, high $CaCO_3$ concentrations in the bottom sediments occur even at great depth. This is the case in the sediments along the eastward path of the Gulf Stream at about 40°N and beneath the area of oceanic upwelling off the coast of southwest Africa. (3) In contrast, the Argentine Basin, where ocean surface organic productivity is also high, shows a virtual absence of calcium carbonate in the bottom sediments at any depth.

FIGURE 3–1 *Pteropod tests from the South Atlantic. Pteropods are molluscs (snails) that deposit aragonitic shells. These shells are easily seen in deep-sea cores because of their relatively large size (about 1 to 2 milimeters). They are not found in sediments raised from water depths greater than 3,500 meters. (Specimens courtesy Dr. C. Chen, Lamont Geological Observatory of Columbia University.)*

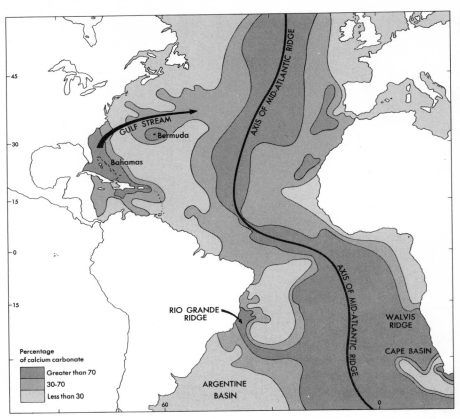

FIGURE 3-2 *The distribution of calcium carbonate on the deep ocean floor of the Atlantic Ocean. The highest values are associated with the ridges and areas of high biological productivity such as the Cape Basin and along the Gulf Stream. The high concentrations around Bermuda and Bahamas are due to shallow-water deposits. (After Turekian, 1964.)*

This pattern is repeated in the East Pacific Ocean (Fig. 3–3). Here the sediments of the East Pacific Rise are high in calcium carbonate as are the sediments under the highly productive waters along the East Pacific Equatorial current. But in the North Pacific Ocean, the sediments are low in calcium carbonate, as in the Argentine Basin. In general, however, with increasing depth there is a gradual decrease in calcium carbonate until about 4,500 meters. At depths greater than this, the concentration drops to extremely low average values (Fig. 3–4). The point at which the calcium carbonate concentration of deep-sea sediments decreases rapidly with depth is commonly called the "compensation depth." At this depth the rate of supply of calcium carbonate is ideally just compensated by an equal rate of solution. The "compensation depth," of course, has little meaning in the areas of extremely high or extremely low calcium carbonate accumulation discussed above, but for major parts of the ocean basin it is a real phenomenon requiring some explanation.

At depths greater than 500 meters, to judge from laboratory experiments, sea water is apparently undersaturated with respect to calcium carbonate, so

Deep-sea sediments

FIGURE 3–3 *The distribution of calcium carbonate on the deep ocean floor of the east Pacific Ocean. Similarly to the Atlantic Ocean, the highest values are associated with ridges and areas of high biological productivity such as the east equatorial Pacific. (After Bramlette, 1961, in* Oceanography, *ed. by Sears.)*

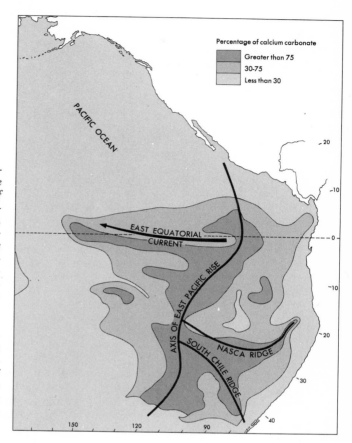

FIGURE 3–4 *The distribution of calcium carbonate in the tops of deep-sea sediment cores as a function of depth of water. The curves connect average values for 1,000-meter intervals for the Atlantic and 500-meter intervals for the Pacific. The "compensation depth" is the approximate depth at which the restricted accumulation of calcium carbonate results in a sharp decreasing trend in calcium carbonate concentration with depth. It is deeper in the mid-Atlantic region than in the deep Pacific. The form of the curve for all data in the deep Atlantic reflects in part the large variations in the rates of clay accumulation as well as the simple depth effect on calcium carbonate accumulation. (After Bramlette, 1961, and Turekian, 1964.)*

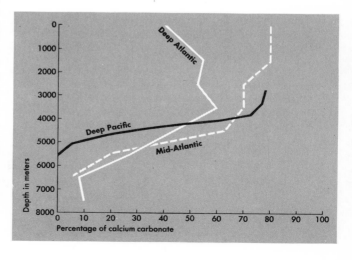

that the compound should dissolve. Hence if the compensation depth were purely the point at which calcium carbonate ought to disappear into solution, the critical level would be 500 meters, not 4,500 meters. Yet the foraminiferans whose tests are commonly found in deep-sea sediments (Fig. 3–5) are those individuals that, despite the dissolving effect of undersaturation, continued to grow a large part of their shells at depths greater than 1,000 meters, as is indicated by the capture of these organisms in deep-sea tows. Further, calcium carbonate in deep-sea sediments is composed not only of thick foraminiferan tests but also of coccoliths. The unicellular plants that produce the coccoliths can only live in the top 100 meters because they depend on light for photosynthesis. Obviously, then, even without continual deposition of calcium carbonate the calcareous tests of these organisms are, at least in part, preserved from dissolving while falling through undersaturated ocean water. Since the organic coatings on the shells constitute a barrier to attack, they may enable some calcium carbonate to reach the bottom. On the basis of settling velocities, we know that the tests of organisms drop through the water fairly rapidly compared to the period of their exposure on the sea floor. Perhaps, then, some property of the bottom will help us understand the "compensation depth."

FIGURE 3–5 *A cross-section of a pelagic foraminiferan test, showing two layers of growth. The thin layer deposited by the young organism in surface waters is added to at depth to form a thick test, typical of the kind found in deep-sea sediments. The channels through the secondary calcite layer are the sites of the pseudopods of the organism. Magnification x 91. (Courtesy Alan Bé, Lamont Geological Observatory.)*

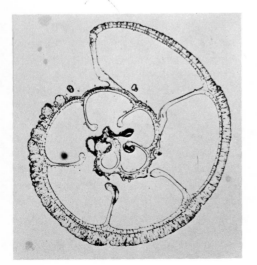

One model of such bottom control of calcium carbonate solution runs as follows: Bottom-dwelling organisms produce CO_2 by respiration. The addition of CO_2 to bottom waters causes the departure from saturation relative to calcium carbonate to increase. Generally, the greater the degree of undersaturation the more rapid the rate of solution of the soluble compound, thus accelerating the solution of the calcium carbonate shells on the ocean floor. This effect will be further enhanced as calcite grains are bared by bottom organisms using the organic coating material for food. Since there is some solution of calcium carbonate as the particles fall through the increasingly undersaturated water there will be less calcium carbonate reaching the deeper parts of the oceans except in areas of very high organic productivity. The already low calcium carbonate concentration is further diminished by the action of bottom organisms, as just described.

Deep-sea sediments

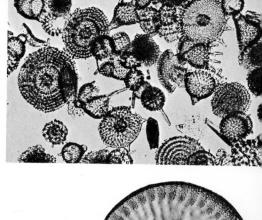

Whatever the reason for the calcium carbonate pattern in the deep-sea sediments, it is clearly associated in some way with depth of water. Recently some investigators have been trying to observe the solution of calcite at different depths in the ocean using accurately weighed crystals of calcite precisely located along a wire let out over the side of the ship. The initial results indicate that the crystals dissolve more rapidly at depths greater than about 3,800 meters than at shallower depths. Perhaps other such experiments at sea combined with the laboratory data will ultimately help us understand the compensation depth.

Silica

There are four groups of organisms that deposit siliceous tests found in deep-sea sediments: diatoms, radiolaria, sponges, and silicoflagellates (Fig. 3-6). The most important of these, in terms of quantity, are diatoms and radiolaria.

Since silica, in the form deposited by these organisms, is highly soluble in sea water, the accumulation of tests on the ocean floor depends on how easily a test is dissolved on its descent through the ocean. The rate of solution depends on the size of the test, the concentration of silica in the water column, and the protective chemical bondings with organic compounds or elements such as magnesium of the test surface.

Siliceous sediments are found mainly at high latitudes and in the equatorial Pacific. Large diatom tests accumulate rapidly at high latitudes

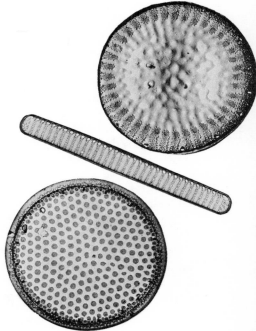

FIGURE 3-6 *Radiolarians (top) and diatoms (bottom) are the most common silica-depositing organisms in the oceans. "Diatomaceous earth," obtained from ancient marine deposits now uplifted and exposed on land, is used commercially as a mild abrasive and in filters for purifying chemicals. (All about 0.1 millimeter diameter.) (Courtesy Carolina Biological Supply Company, and P. E. Hargraves, Lamont Geological Observatory.)*

during the summer seasons; in the equatorial Pacific the efficient growth of diatoms and radiolaria occurs because of a good supply of nutrients and silica from the upwelling of deeper phosphate- and silica-rich waters.

Deep-sea sediments

Phosphatic and Organic Material

Since the bones of most vertebrates are composed mainly of the mineral apatite $(Ca_5(PO_4)_3OH)$, and since the bone debris of fish and marine mammals are likely to sink, we would anticipate finding phosphatic deposits on the sea floor. Contrary to expectation, however, very little skeletal phosphate reaches the deep ocean bottom, for either the effect of pressure on increasing the solubility of apatite and other phosphate compounds or the efficiency of biological cycling prevents preservation of the bones and other phosphatic debris during their descent through the water. Fish debris, shark teeth, and ear bones of whales have been found in deep-sea sediments, but these occurrences, although interesting, are minor in terms of the total sedimentation in the deep oceans.

Organic compounds produced by life processes likewise are less abundant in deep-sea sediments than might be predicted from the amount produced in surface waters. Most of the organic compounds are utilized as food before they reach the bottom. Despite this extraction, however, enough reaches the bottom to support a sizeable fauna of worms, serpent stars (echinoderms), holothuria, and molluscs, to name the major groups (Fig. 3–7).

Organic material accumulates more readily in sediments where the overlying water is deficient in oxygen. Most of the ocean basins have plenty of dissolved oxygen that can be used for the metabolism of organic compounds by aerobic (or molecular-oxygen-using) organisms. This supply is available because there is a relatively rapid turnover of the oceans and well-aerated waters penetrate to the deepest parts of the oceans.

FIGURE 3–7 *Pictures taken of the ocean bottom of the Antarctic Ocean showing the diverse kinds of bottom-dwelling life and their trails. These include worms, serpent stars, and holothuria. (Courtesy H. G. Goodell, Florida State University.)*

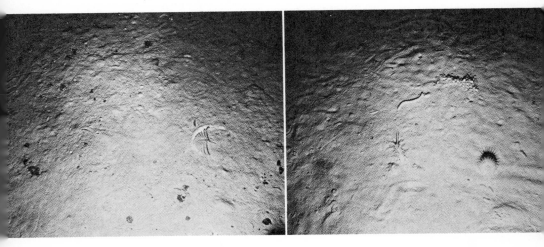

Some local basins, however, can become isolated from the main deep-water circulation, and there the oxygen is used up so rapidly that the level always remains extremely low. These are called stagnant basins. Although anaerobic bacteria can make use of combined (nonmolecular) oxygen to metabolize organic material, the process is considerably less efficient than the process of aerobic metabolism, and consequently more organic material accumulates in the sediments.

The Black Sea and the Cariaco Trench off Venezuela are essentially anaerobic basins of this sort and the concentration of organic material in the sediments is as high as 3 to 5 per cent. The Argentine Basin, on the other hand, has as much as 5 per cent organic material in the sediments even though the oxygen level is not very low. This difference can be explained if either the organic compounds present are not easily metabolized by common marine organisms or if the rate of supply is greater than the rate of usage by bottom-dwelling organisms. On the whole, however, the organic-compound concentration in deep-sea sediments is less than 1 per cent.

Nonbiogenic Components

Clay Minerals

In the distribution of clay minerals in deep-sea sediments we encounter the three nonbiogenic components: the pelagic, the bottom-transported, and the indigenous.

Clay sedimentation in the Atlantic Ocean is almost entirely influenced by continental sources. Figure 3–8, for instance, shows the variation of the kaolinite/chlorite ratio in the Atlantic Ocean. This ratio is particularly informative because it represents the maximal effect of climatic zones on weathering products. Kaolinite is typical of weathering in tropical climates, conditions under which chlorite is easily destroyed. Weathering in temperate and arctic environments results in the preservation or formation of chlorite. Thus, there is a sharp decrease in the kaolinite/chlorite ratio with increasing latitude.

The Pacific Ocean is rimmed by deep trenches that trap bottom-transported material from the continents. This is so at the present time, but in the past, continuous canyons and other avenues of transport down the continental rise must have existed in the northeast Pacific basin to result in the large abyssal plains in that area.

Pelagic detrital sedimentation (as defined in Table 3–1) occurs throughout most of the Pacific Ocean, but its importance relative to indigenous components (as defined in Table 3–1) diminishes near the center of the Pacific where volcanic activity has been prominent. This is best seen in the relative abundance of the clay mineral illite (or detrital mica), clearly derived from

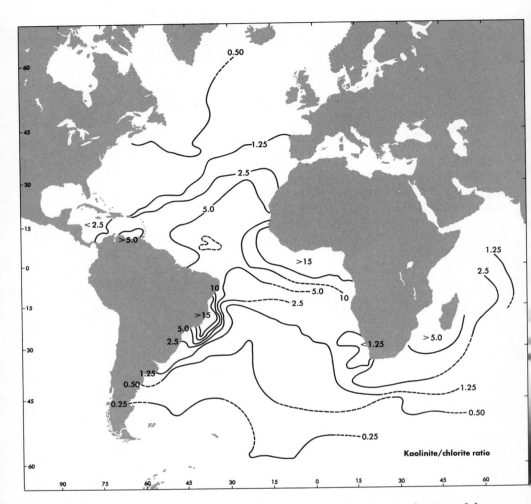

FIGURE 3–8 *The kaolinite/chlorite ratio variation in the clay-size fraction of deep-sea sediments of the Atlantic Ocean. Kaolinite is formed in intensely weathered soils typical of the equatorial region. The pattern in the sediments reflects the weathering intensity on the adjacent continents. The ratio of kaolinite to chlorite is actually the ratio of intensities of X-ray diffraction peaks. (After Biscaye, 1965.)*

land, to the other minerals of the Pacific deep-sea sediments (Fig. 3–9). The most prominent of these other minerals is montmorillonite which is closely associated with the zeolite phillipsite (see p. 45). Both of these minerals in the Pacific are probably the reaction products of hydrated basaltic glass (palagonite), supplied from local, probably submarine, volcanoes, with sea water; hence they represent unequivocal indigenous components.

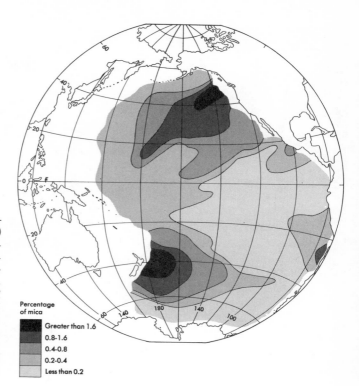

FIGURE 3-9 *The distribution of illite (or detrital mica) in the Pacific Ocean deepsea sediments. The percentages are of total minerals other than biologically derived calcium carbonate and silica. Mica is obviously derived from land and may be primarily transported by winds. (From G. Arrhenius, International Conference on Earth Science, MIT, 1964.)*

Percentage
of mica

■	Greater than 1.6
■	0.8-1.6
	0.4-0.8
	0.2-0.4
	Less than 0.2

Quartz and Other Detrital Minerals

Quartz is a significant detrital component of the Atlantic Ocean sediments (Fig. 3–10). Except for some windblown sand off northwest Africa, the largest amount of fine-size quartz is found in pelagic sediments at the high latitudes. These may be attributed to the pulverizing action of the glaciers of Antarctica and Greenland during transport to the ocean margin.

In the Pacific Ocean two prominent sources appear to be: (1) the North American continent, the greatest concentration (relative to all silicate minerals) lying off the coast of Washington and Oregon, and (2) New Zealand, the concentration decreasing eastward. The distribution east of New Zealand may be attributed at least in part to wind transport, because of the prevailing westerlies, but it is more difficult to make a case for wind transport in the Northern Hemisphere occurrence.

In addition to quartz, other minerals such as feldspars and amphiboles also occur in deep-sea sediments, especially in the silt-size fraction. These can be derived either from the continents or from sources found within the ocean basins.

Gibbsite, the hydrated aluminum oxide, deserves special mention. The common end product of intense tropical weathering, it is a principle component of the most important aluminum ore, bauxite. Its distribution in deep-

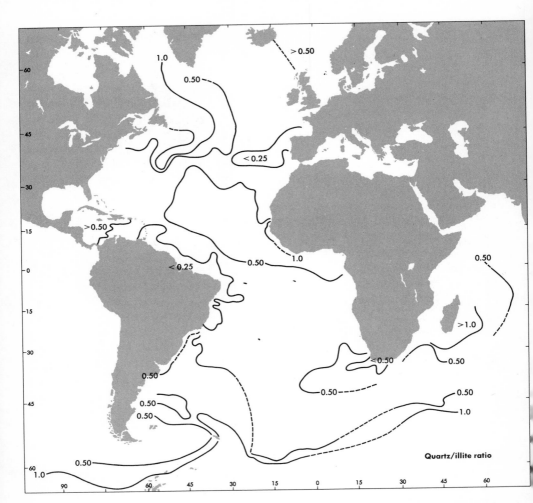

FIGURE 3-10 *The quartz-illite ratio variation in the fine silt-size fraction of deep-sea sediments of the Atlantic Ocean. The high quartz content off the Sahara probably represents wind-borne material (see Fig 2-7). The high quartz at the high latitudes is due to the supply of ground quartz-bearing rock by glaciers from Greenland and Antarctica. The ratio of quartz to illite is actually the ratio of intensities of X-ray diffraction peaks. (After Biscaye, 1965.)*

sea sediments is similar to that of kaolinite, for it occurs where continent-derived materials are dominant, as in the Atlantic Ocean.

Volcanic Products

Three types of volcanic material exist on the ocean bottom: rock fragments, volcanic glass, and minerals produced by the action of volcanic material with hot water. Since volcanic islands are predominantly basaltic in composition, it is not surprising that by far the most common rock fragments found by dredging the ocean bottom are basalts. These samples are found mainly on the oceanic ridges and seamounts. Volcanic glass found in deep-sea deposits is also primarily basaltic, although pumice (a glass more granitic in composition) is not uncommon. Basaltic glass exists either in the relatively unhydrated form called hyaloclastite or in the hydrated form, palagonite. The hyaloclastite appears to be stable for long periods of time, but in sea water the palagonite devitrifies to form both the zeolite phillipsite and montmorillonite (Fig. 3–11).

The zeolite minerals in the deep-sea sediments are presumed to be derived

FIGURE 3–11 *Basaltic glass with needles of the zeolite, phillipsite, radiating from it. It is believed that phillipsite and montmorillonite are formed by the devitrification of hydrated basaltic glass. Magnification x 190. (Courtesy E. Bonatti, University of Miami.)*

indigenously. The zeolites are framework-type silicates, many of which have strong ion-exchange or water and volatile adsorption capacities. They commonly occur as late-stage products of hot-water activity in volcanic areas. The most common zeolite in the Pacific Ocean sediments is potassium-rich phillipsite, which may constitute more than half of the sediment in areas with a low rate of clay accumulation and a high rate of volcanic activity. A map of phillipsite distribution in the Pacific is reproduced in Fig. 3–12. In sharp con-

FIGURE 3–12 *The distribution of the zeolite, phillipsite, in the Pacific Ocean deep-sea sediments. It is clearly related to areas of high volcanic activity in the middle of the Pacific Ocean, where it can make up more than 50 per cent of the silicate minerals in the sediments. The dashed lines are estimated boundaries where data do not exist. Phillipsite is very rare in the Atlantic Ocean. (After Bonatti, 1963.)*

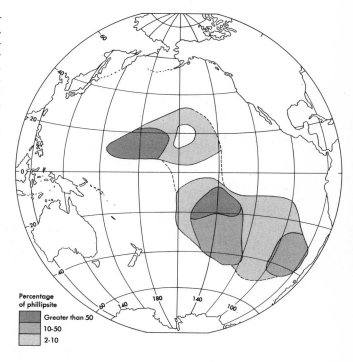

Percentage of phillipsite

Greater than 50

10-50

2-10

trast, sediments in the Atlantic Ocean and western Indian Ocean and the Antarctic Ocean contain virtually no phillipsite. Common there is heulandite (or clinoptilolite), a sodium-calcium zeolite which appears to be most abundant at high latitudes.

Manganese Nodules

Concretions, coatings, or nodules of hydrous manganese and iron oxides are a common feature of the deep-sea floor. The occurrence may range from coatings on minerals or coccoliths ($< 30\mu$) to discrete nodules up to 850 kilograms in mass. Table 3-2 gives the average composition of manganese nodules. In the formation of nodules, manganese and iron accrete in concentric layers, sometimes mixed with foreign material such as clay, calcium

Table 3-2

Average Composition of Manganese Nodules

Element	Weight Percentages (Dry-Weight Basis)		Element	Weight Percentages (Dry-Weight Basis)	
	Pacific Ocean	Atlantic Ocean		Pacific Ocean	Atlantic Ocean
B	0.029	0.03	Fe	14.0	17.5
Na	2.6	2.3	Co	0.35	0.31
Mg	1.7	1.7	Ni	0.99	0.42
Al	2.9	3.1	Cu	0.53	0.20
Si	9.4	11.0	Sr	0.081	0.09
K	0.8	0.7	Y	0.016	0.018
Ca	1.9	2.7	Zr	0.063	0.054
Sc	0.001	0.002	Mo	0.052	0.035
Ti	0.67	0.8	Ba	0.18	0.17
V	0.054	0.07	Yb	0.0031	0.004
Cr	0.001	0.002	Pb	0.09	0.10
Mn	24.2	16.3			

After Mero, 1961.

carbonate, or volcanic debris. Manganese nodules have been found by dredging and by underwater photography in most parts of the oceans (Fig. 3–13). They are, however, most common in areas with low accumulation rates of clay and calcium carbonate, specifically, (1) areas scoured by bottom currents such as submarine hills and regions like the Drake Passage between Antarctica and South America and the Blake Plateau off the southeastern United States, and (2) areas of pelagic clay deposition such as the central Pacific Ocean (Fig. 3–14).

The source of the elements for the nodules is probably twofold: (1) detrital manganese and iron oxides from the continents, and (2) manganese and iron derived from the reaction of submarine volcanic products with sea water.

Deep-sea sediments

46

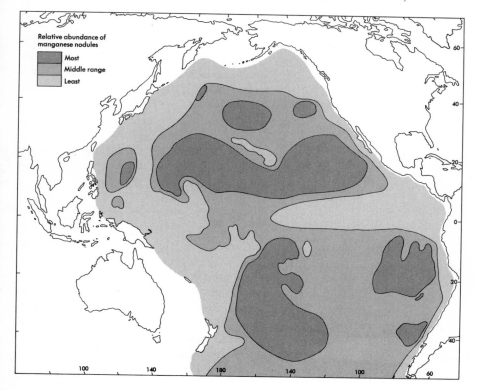

FIGURE 3–13 *A section through a manganese nodule dredged from the Atlantic Ocean floor showing a core or nucleus of volcanic rock. Other materials may act as nuclei of manganese nodules including shark teeth, ear bones of whales, and even naval artillery shells. Scale equals 1 centimeter.*

FIGURE 3–14 *The relative distribution of manganese nodules on the Pacific Ocean floor from the estimates of Soviet scientists. A similar general pattern may exist for the Atlantic Ocean. The ridge areas, or areas under strong surface biological productivity, where the sediments are rich in calcium carbonate, do not appear to have high concentrations of manganese nodules. (After Skornyakova and Andruchenko, 1964.)*

Relative abundance of
manganese nodules

Most

Middle range

Least

The nodules and concretions grow at various rates. For instance, coatings of manganese oxide can be seen on very recently deposited pteropod tests in deep-sea sediments. A twentieth-century naval artillery shell dredged from the continental margin off California had developed layers, several inches thick, with a high ratio of iron to manganese. Nodules from the deep-sea, however, indicate growth rates slower than 5 millimeters per million years, as determined by means of radioactive dating.

Nodules appear to be lying at the interface between water and sediment but some underwater photographs indicate that sediments may cover over large areas of manganese nodules. And to judge from a number of successful recoveries of nodules from cores, they occur in the sediment at least as deep as one meter.

The formation of a manganese nodule requires a supply of manganese in solution and a nucleus, such as a rock fragment or bone debris, around which the manganese can precipitate out of solution when its supply exceeds the saturation concentration. Manganese ions can exist in several oxidation states, as Mn^{+2} and Mn^{+4}. The formation of manganese nodules implies a supply of reduced Mn^{+2} in solution which becomes oxidized to the Mn^{+4} state on contact with oxygen-rich sea water and then is precipitated. There are two possible sources of reduced manganese (Mn^{+2}): (1) It can be derived from volcanic basalt at the ocean bottom in which most of the iron and manganese would be in their reduced states. On reaction with sea water the volcanic material would release manganese as Mn^{+2}, which would be oxidized and precipitated as MnO_2. (2) Oxidized manganese, as MnO_2, transported from land as detritus and buried in deep-sea sediments with organic material, can be reduced by organisms living in the sediment. The manganese as Mn^{+2} would then migrate through interstitial waters in the sediment, and, on encountering sea water, would be oxidized to Mn^{+4} and precipitated.

At present the surest clue to which mechanism is operating, if indeed one alone must be invoked, is to consider the associated materials. The presence of submarine volcanic debris, including basaltic glass, phillipsite, and montmorillonite, would favor the basaltic supply of manganese. The absence of obvious volcanic association would favor the detrital supply.

Trace Elements

The minerals discussed above are composed mainly of the major rock-forming elements—Na, K, Mg, Ca, Si, Al. The remaining 90 per cent of the metallic elements of the periodic chart are the *minor*, or *trace*, metallic *elements*. Their presence in deep-sea sediments is controlled by the supply from the continents and from indigenous sources. The clay minerals and oxides from the continents have trace elements incorporated into the crystal lattices and adsorbed to the surfaces. Since smaller particles have larger surfaces per unit of mass than larger particles, sediments composed of a large proportion

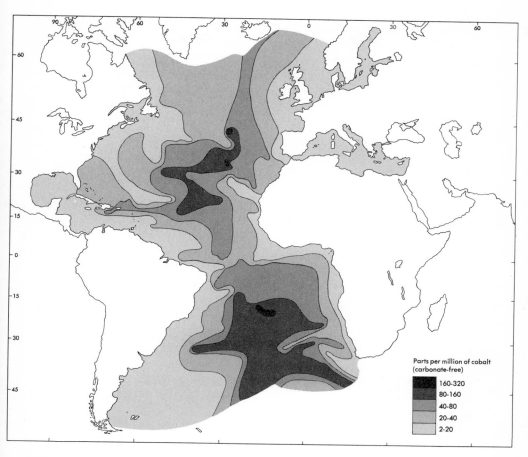

Parts per million of cobalt
(carbonate-free)

■	160-320
▨	80-160
▧	40-80
░	20-40
□	2-20

FIGURE 3–15 *The distribution of cobalt in deep-sea sediments of the Atlantic Ocean (on a calcium-carbonate-free basis) showing that the high concentrations are associated with the mid-Atlantic ridge area and the low concentrations are associated with the abyssal plain areas. (After Turekian and Imbrie, 1966.)*

of small particles will have a high concentration of some trace elements. Figure 3–15 is a map of the concentration of cobalt in the tops of deep-sea sediment cores from the Atlantic Ocean, calculated to a calcium carbonate-free basis (that is, assuming the cobalt is associated with the non-calcium carbonate fraction of the sediments). In the abyssal plains, where the bottom-transported, relatively coarse-grained materials are deposited, the cobalt concentration is low, whereas on the "hilltops" of the Mid-Atlantic Ridge where only fine-grained pelagic detrital material is deposited, the concentrations are high.

Trace elements may also occur in marine organisms as specific compounds, such as copper in hemocyanin in the blood of crustacea, and they may be

Deep-sea sediments

adsorbed on the phosphatic tests of the zooplankton or embedded as micro-crystals in the protoplasm of microorganisms. Table 3–3 shows the concentrations of some trace elements in plankton from the North Atlantic Ocean. As shown above, very little phosphate reaches the deep-sea bottom; consequently, we should expect very little transport of trace elements, in association with invertebrate phosphatic material, to the ocean bottom.

Table 3–3

The Composition of the Ash of Plankton
from the North Atlantic Ocean

Sample Number	Percentage		Sr	Pb	Parts per Million		Ni	Ag
	Ca	Mg			Sn	Cr		
3	26.7	9.70	5800	340	22	370	430	0.4
4	20.6	10.51	4600	64	24	860	610	0.3
5	21.2	7.75	3500	48	7	38	25	2.8
6	18.8	5.95	2700	15	19	52	59	3.0
7	18.8	5.86	2800	240	10	78	94	2.0
8	23.6	4.29	2400	450	16	122	46	1.8
9	38.6	3.88	3300	530	5	19	52	1.8
10	23.4	5.60	6200	376	< 5	24	15	0.2
11	21.8	5.86	6500	222	< 5	10	14	0.3
12	9.4	4.43	1100	38	14	90	70	2.4

3 is composed mainly of crustacea, 10 and 11 are composed mainly of *Sargassum*, 4–7 are sub-arctic species, 8–9 are warm species.

4

Stratigraphy and geochronometry
of deep-sea deposits

Sediments accumulate under the force of gravity and form deposits that are parallel with the ocean surface. At any particular location, if the record has not been disturbed by slumping, the downward sequence is a sequence back in time. If there are changes in the color, texture, mineralogy, paleontology, or any other property, the sediments are said to be layered; the study of layering is called *stratigraphy*.

In the deep ocean the stratigraphic record is obtained by means of coring devices of the type shown in Fig. 4–1. These are simple tubes that penetrate the sediment either by gravity alone ("gravity-coring") or with the aid of a piston as shown ("piston-coring"). Of the two, the latter permits the deeper penetration—up to 20 meters. Recently the techniques of coring by means of rotary drills, similar to those used in oil-drilling ventures on the continental shelf, have been used in deeper water. Near Guadalupe Island, for instance, the preliminary Mohole drilling, performed in 10,000 feet of water, reached 500 feet into the sediments.

The object of deep-sea stratigraphic studies is to relate the sequence of sediments at a particular location to: (1) sequences elsewhere in the ocean in order to determine horizontal variations in sediment pattern at a particular time, (2) world-wide climatic events, (3) oceanic circulation patterns and their variations with time, and (4) events on the continents.

With the advent of methods of absolute dating by means of radioactivity, much of the stratigraphic record can be compared with contemporaneous world-wide events. Radioactive dating also permits us to determine the accumulation rates of the various deep-sea sediment components. This information is important especially in understanding the fate of the elements brought to the sea by streams and the general history of ocean basins.

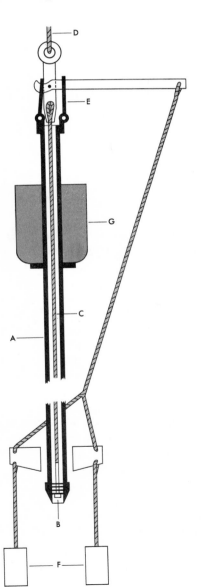

The Stratigraphy of Nonbiogenic Components

By using lithological, mineralogical, and geophysical observations, we can gain stratigraphic information from the nonbiogenic components of deep-sea sediments. This procedure has proven particularly valuable in the correlation of glacial deposits, volcanic deposits, and the mineralogical and geophysical properties (such as magnetism) of the clay-size fraction of the deep-sea sediments with large-scale and even world-wide events.

FIGURE 4–1 *A diagram of a piston corer. A is the coring tube. B is a snugly fitting piston that is connected to the cable, D, by means of a strong wire, C. When the counterweights, F, touch the bottom a release mechanism, E, from which the coring tube is suspended is activated and the tube drops rapidly in free fall. The weight, G, gives the falling tube enough energy to be driven into the sediment over the piston. The sediments are sucked into the tube by the piston as the tube penetrates the sediment layers, resulting in a relatively undisturbed stratified section of the sediments of the ocean floor. A piston corer can be used to obtain cores as long as 20 meters. (After Dietrich, 1963.)*

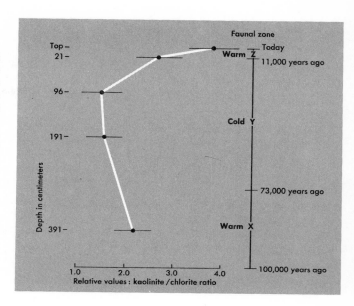

FIGURE 4–2 *The variation of the kaolinite/chlorite ratio with depth in the 2- to 20-micron fraction of an Atlantic equatorial deep-sea core (Lamont A180–74). The length of the line through each point represents the error of measurement. The low kaolinite/chlorite ratios correspond to glacial times and are correlated with higher rates of clay accumulations relative to postglacial times. The faunal zones X, Y, and Z correspond to warm, cold, and warm times respectively. (Courtesy P. E. Biscaye.)*

Lithological and Mineralogical Correlations

Lithologically, for example, it has been possible to distinguish between glacial and nonglacial deposits, especially in the Arctic and the Antarctic. In cores raised from regions where icebergs are very common today, below a certain level ice-rafted material is absent, thus indicating the local onset of massive glaciation in these areas. This event occurred about 2.5 million years ago, as we shall see later, and may mark a critical point in the general cooling of the Earth's climate resulting in the "glacial age."

Changes in the mineralogy and rates of accumulation of clay occur in the deep-sea sediments if the relative importance of different sources has changed with time. Thus, during glacial times, the change in sea level and possibly the increased sediment load carried by mountain streams resulted in higher rates of clay accumulation in the equatorial mid-Atlantic region than at present. The glacial times are reflected in the deep-sea sediments of this region by the greater amount of chlorite relative to kaolinite (Fig. 4–2).

Layers of volcanic material are often found in deep-sea sediment cores. If the volcanism was extensive enough the layer of debris may be followed for hundreds of miles. For example, ash layers have been found in the eastern Mediterranean that correspond to major eruptions of the Santorini volcano near Crete. Each major eruption deposited fine-grained glass of a specific composition and thus can be identified in the deep-sea sediments (Fig. 4–3).

Magnetic-Reversal Correlation

Recently, what appears to be the most useful correlative property on a world-wide basis has been discovered—the periodic reversal of the Earth's

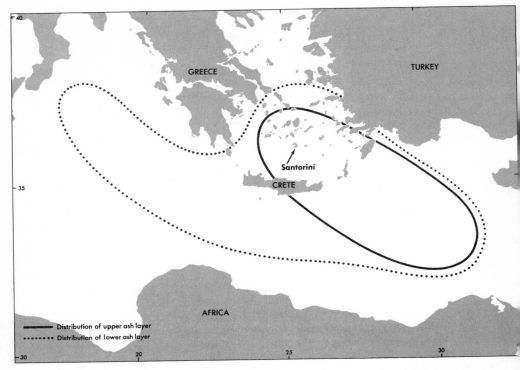

FIGURE 4–3   *The extent of volcanic ash distributions of two distinguishable explosions in the eastern Mediterranean as recorded in deep-sea cores. The lower ash layer occurred in prehistoric times (greater than 25,000 years ago) while the upper layer is less than 5,000 years old. Both ash layers are ascribed to the explosive eruption of Santorini in the Aegean Sea. The ash layers are correlated by the distinctive index of refraction of the glass derived from a particular event. The index of refraction, determined with a microscope on small glass fragments, is related to the chemical composition of the glass. The lower layer has an index of refraction of 1.521 and the upper layer has an index of refraction of 1.509. Volcanic glass with the same index of refraction as the upper layer has been found extensively on islands which are parts of the original volcanic island. The upper layer ash may be related to a dramatic event in the Aegean which gave rise to the legend of Atlantis.*
(*After Ninkovich and Heezen, 1967.*)

polarity (Fig. 4–4). It has been observed in volcanic sequences on land that the north and south poles of the Earth's magnetic field have reversed fairly frequently. The evidence is supplied by the strongly magnetic iron oxide minerals in basaltic rocks, which retain the magnetic polarity in force at the time of cooling. For instance, our present polarity began 700,000 years ago, and before that, for about 2 million years, the poles were reversed except for two small episodes of "normal" polarity (Fig. 4–5).

The sequence of orientation of the magnetic poles observed in volcanic rocks on land is also recorded by the iron oxide fraction of deep-sea sediments. The orientation of magnets in the Earth's magnetic field can be resolved into a horizontal and a verticle component. That is, the north pole of a freely swinging magnet will point in the horizontal plane to the Earth's south mag-

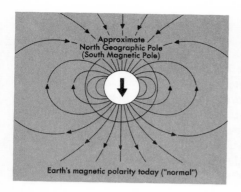 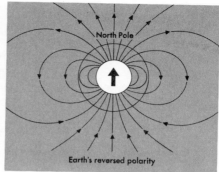

FIGURE 4–4 *The Earth as a magnet. The north magnetic pole of the Earth at the present time is found in the vicinity of the south geographic pole. That is why the north poles of magnets point north following the lines of force of the Earth magnet. The reversed polarity (relative to the present) occurs when the north magnetic pole and the north geographic pole are coincident.*

FIGURE 4–5 *The reversal of the Earth's magnetic field with time was established by determining the magnetic polarity of volcanic materials, whose ages were determined by potassium-argon dating. These figures have been established on materials from many parts of the world. (From "Reversals of the Earth's Magnetic Field," Cox, Dalrymple, and Doell. Copyright © 1967 by Scientific American, Inc. All rights reserved.)*

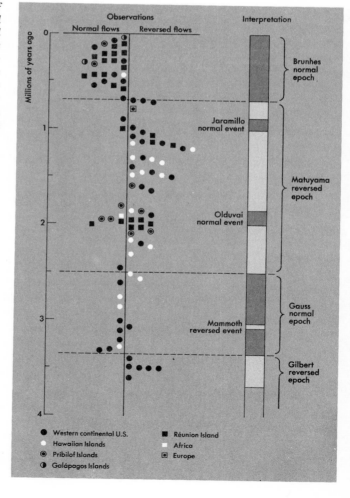

netic pole and be inclined vertically in the direction of the lines of force. Because commonly used coring techniques do not give reliable information on horizontal orientation of the core, polarity can be ascertained only where the magnetic lines of force have relatively steep vertical components. The stratification in the core will, however, give a correct indication of the plane of the horizontal. As seen in Fig. 4–4 the vertical component is greatest at high latitudes and approaches zero around the equator. Hence a magnetic vector pointing up, relative to the horizontal stratification of the core, indicates an opposite polarity to a magnetic vector pointing down in the same core. The results obtained by this method are shown in Fig. 4–15. The method cannot be used, however, if there is any question of the continuity of sedimentation in the core or if distinctive paleontologic markers are lacking, since we are dealing with a flip-flop type of record that does not have singular properties.

The Stratigraphy of Biogenic Components

In deep-sea sediments there are three possible types of correlations by fossils: (1) the relative abundance of tests of different species as indicators of the temperature of water or the appearance of new species and the disappearance of old ones, (2) the variation in biogenic calcium carbonate and silica concentrations as indicators of oceanic mixing rates and nutrient supply, and (3) the variation in the relative abundance of oxygen isotopes in calcareous material as a function of water temperature or salinity. We will consider important examples of each of these three major types.

Fossil Abundances

The relative abundance of certain species or subspecies of foraminiferans has been used in correlation, especially in the upper parts of sediment cores. Variations in abundance of these fossils represent fluctuations of climate due to continental glaciation, and thus provide a means of estimating the relative temperature of the surface of the oceans. In particular the abundance of *Globorotalia menardii* has been used as an indicator of coldness and warmness and has been correlated throughout the Atlantic Ocean and Caribbean for the last 100,000 years, a period during which the continental ice fluctuated considerably (Fig. 4–6).

The extinction of a group of organisms called *Discoasters*, which most closely resemble the coccoliths, has been used as an important stratigraphic point correlated in all the oceans. It possibly represents a major event in the oceans more than a million years ago during the Pleistocene glacial age.

Similar correlations have been made with the radiolarians, especially in the Antarctic, where the transition from relatively warm to cold surface ocean conditions took place when glaciation became massive on the continent. The warm-water species drop out in the Antarctic Ocean and are replaced by cold-water species just at the time when ice-rafted deposits and diatom deposits became important.

Variations in the Abundance of Calcium Carbonate and Silica

The calcium carbonate concentration of deep-sea sediments is a function of the relative accumulation rates of clay and calcium carbonate. If the clay accumulation rate in an area is sensibly constant, then changes in the calcium carbonate concentration can be ascribed to changes in its accumulation rate.

FIGURE 4–6 *Atlantic and Caribbean deep-sea cores showing variations in climate as reflected by: (1) the relative abundance of a foraminiferan* Globorotalia menardii *(left of each pair)—a large abundance corresponding to warm conditions; and (2) the oxygen isotopic composition variation of another foraminiferan species occurring throughout the core—*Globigerinoides sacculifera. *The symbols C and W stand for "cold" and "warm" respectively as inferred from G. menardii abundances. The temperature scale is given in centigrade. This may not reflect actual ocean-surface temperatures alone but may be the variation of oxygen-18-to-oxygen-16 ratios as a result of isotopic fractionation during ice storage on continental glaciers. The correlation between the two independent methods is good back through about 120,000 years. The ages given are radiocarbon ages determined on the foraminiferans and are given as years before the present time. (After Ericson et al., 1961. The oxygen isotopic data are taken from Emiliani, 1955.)*

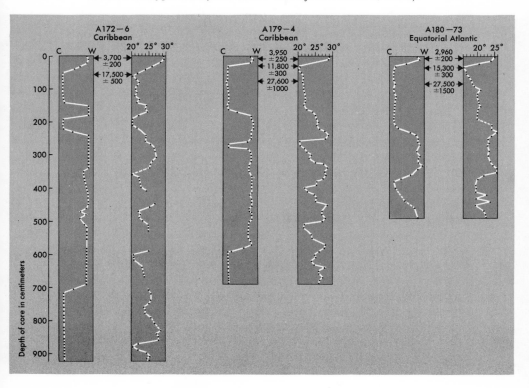

In the North Atlantic, under the present location of the Gulf Stream, there is a band of high calcium carbonate concentration in postglacial deep-sea sediments (see Chapter 3). This deposit is related to high biological productivity associated with the Gulf Stream. In the past, in response to glacial conditions, the Gulf Stream coursed eastward at a lower latitude, so calcium carbonate deposition was considerably lower under the present location of the Gulf Stream. Hence, the calcium carbonate concentration curve in Fig. 4–7 indicates lower values during glacial times than in postglacial or interglacial times.

In the Gulf of Mexico the end of the last glacial period 11,000 years ago is marked in deep-sea sediments by a sudden transition in composition. Turbidity-current deposits, which derived from the Mississippi delta that had been exposed by the lowered sea level characteristic of glacial times, diminished drastically at the end of glaciation. Almost pure deep-sea calcium carbonate deposits, which are undiluted by detrital material from the continent, have been accumulating since then.

Similar examples of the control exerted by climate on the calcium carbonate concentration in deep-sea cores are found in the Pacific Ocean. In the

FIGURE 4–7 *A core (A164–15) raised from the North Atlantic Basin under the general area of the Gulf Stream. The high-calcium-carbonate segments of the core correspond to times of warm climates and the low-calcium-carbonate-concentration segments correspond to glacial times, as indicated by the abundance of foraminifera. Z and X correspond to warm times, and Y and W correspond to glacial times. Presumably the presently high calcium carbonate concentration is due to high biological productivity in the region of the Gulf Stream. It follows from this that the low calcium carbonate concentrations occur because the Gulf Stream had shifted from the characteristic location of warm times. The rate of clay accumulation is essentially constant down the length of the core.*

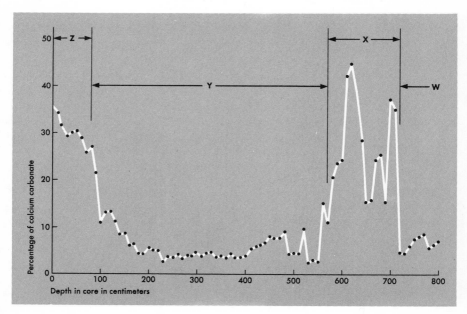

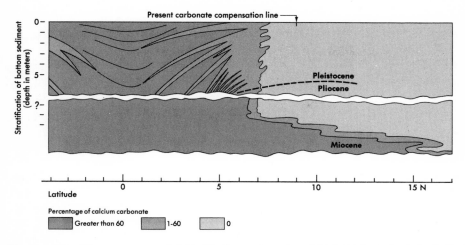

FIGURE 4–8 *The east equatorial Pacific Ocean is a site of high biological productivity because of upwelling produced by trade winds. During glacial times the Earth's climatic zones were "compressed," resulting in more intense winds—especially the trade winds. This led to greater upwelling hence greater productivity and more calcium carbonate deposition on the ocean floor. High calcium carbonate concentrations are thus correlated with glacial times in sediments from the east equatorial Pacific. (After Arrhenius, 1963, in*
The Sea, *ed. by Hill.)*

equatorial Pacific, for example, the time of highest calcium carbonate deposition rate coincided with the greatest trade wind activity; these winds were the result of the contracted atmospheric circulation system due to continental glaciation. The strong easterly winds that drive the equatorial Pacific currents produce shear motions in the surface waters, resulting in increased upwelling; this leads to increased biological productivity and hence greater deposition of calcium carbonate (Fig. 4–8).

Silica distribution in Antarctic cores, as implied above (p. 56), is also strongly related to climate, although the relationship is not yet clear. We know that at the present time the influence of a completely glaciated Antarctic continent is associated with a high level of production and deposition of diatoms in Antarctic waters. The absence of ice-rafted sediments and the presence of warmer-water radiolaria indicate that there was no massive Antarctic ice-cap before 2.5 million years ago (as we discussed above); this "warm" time also shows a very low silica concentration in the sediments, perhaps indicating that the upwelling of waters rich in nutrients and silica was less than now.

Oxygen Isotopes

We normally think of elements such as oxygen, calcium, or carbon as the smallest units useful in describing chemical properties. With the advent of precise instruments like mass spectrometers, we now know that an element can often be resolved into units with slightly different masses called *isotopes*. Isotopes of an element have the same number of protons in the nucleus but different numbers of neutrons. The greater the number of neutrons the greater the mass number of the isotope. Since the differences in mass are small, to a good first approximation the isotopes of an element have identical chemical properties. On closer view, however, it is apparent that the differences in masses between isotopes of an element do affect chemical reactions, since atoms are being transferred from one molecule to another. Energy differences, as dictated by the masses in motion, result in the unequal distribution of the isotopes among the chemical species (or compounds) involved.

To describe the distribution of isotopes among the compounds when equilibrium is attained, we must use the laws of chemical equilibrium described in Chapter 6. Since we are interested mainly in the distribution of the isotopes between two compounds (or states) as a function of temperature, we can restrict ourselves to reactions involving the simple exchange of isotopes between the compounds. In the case of calcium carbonate deposition from sea water, an isotope-exchange reaction can be written for the two common isotopes of oxygen, oxygen-16 (99%) and oxygen-18 (1%), in the following manner:

$$\tfrac{1}{3} CaCO_3^{16} + H_2O^{18} = \tfrac{1}{3} CaCO_3^{18} + H_2O^{16}$$

We use fractions of molecules in order to focus on the exchange of single atoms of oxygen between molecules.

For this reaction the equilibrium constant, K (see Chapter 6), is written:

$$K \text{ (a function of temperature)} = \frac{\text{The product of the number of molecules of each of the products}}{\text{The product of the number of molecules of each of the reactants}} = \frac{(\text{No. molecules } CaCO_3^{18})^{1/3} \times (\text{No. molecules } H_2O^{16})}{(\text{No. molecules } CaCO_3^{16})^{1/3} \times (\text{No. molecules } H_2O^{18})}$$

At equilibrium, calcium carbonate will have a different ratio of isotopes from that of water because the chemical bonds are different for the two molecules. Although the removal of calcium carbonate from solution as a precipitate will alter the isotopic composition of the water, practically speaking, the oceans are so large and homogeneous that essentially no measurable change in the isotopic composition of sea water takes place by the deposition of the calcium carbonate, so that the ratio H_2O^{16}/H_2O^{18} remains sensibly constant. At different temperatures, different amounts of heavy oxygen will, however, be found in the calcium carbonate relative to sea water. Professor Harold C. Urey in 1948 calculated the expected temperature-controlled variation in the process, the results of which are shown in Table 4–1. This information is the basis of paleo-temperature analysis of carbonate shells deposited in ancient seas.

The temperature of the surface waters of the deep-sea varies with latitude, hence foraminiferan tests at different latitudes deposit calcium carbonate that reflects this temperature variation in the ratio of oxygen-18 to oxygen-16. The

Table 4-1

Oxygen-Isotope Fractionation*

Temperature (in °C)	$\frac{O^{18}}{O^{16}}$ Water	$\frac{O^{18}}{O^{16}}$ Crystal
0	$\frac{1}{500}$	$\frac{1.026}{500}$
20	$\frac{1}{500}$	$\frac{1.022}{500}$

*As a function of temperature between water and calcium carbonate; as qualitatively proposed by Professor Urey in 1948.

temperature variations that have occured with time, implied by the paleontologic data, thus will be recorded by the oxygen-isotopic composition of the foraminiferan tests deposited on the sea floor. The oxygen-isotopic compositions vary with depth in deep-sea cores in the same fashion as other climatic indicators (Fig. 4–6), and are compatible with the known climatic changes, as a result of glaciation, recorded in continental deposits.

Another interpretation has been made of the oxygen-isotope variations shown in Fig. 4–6. We have assumed that the isotopic composition of sea water has remained constant with time. Actually, in the transfer of water vapor from the oceans and redeposition on land as snow during glacial times, there would be an increase in the O^{18}/O^{16} ratio of sea water. As Table 4–1 shows, this would appear like a *decrease* in temperature in the analysis of the calcium carbonate shell depositing from the heavier water. In constructing Fig. 4–6 an attempt was made to correct for this. One can imagine that the correction was not great enough and that perhaps the major variation in isotopic composition could be due to changes in the isotopic composition of the sea water as the result of light-water transfer to continental glaciers. If this proves to be the case, the observed isotopic variations will still remain as excellent indicators of glacial age events but not of ocean surface temperatures.

Radioactive Geochronometry

All the stratigraphic techniques discussed above give information that can be fitted into the surface history of the Earth only crudely unless absolute dates are made. Not until the perfection of radioactive methods of dating geologic materials was it possible to get absolute correlations of events over long distances or between the continents and the oceans. These methods also made possible the accurate determination of rates of sediment accumulation or rates of biological evolution.

Radioactivity is the result of adjustment of the nuclei of atoms from unstable to more stable states. In the process, energetic particles are ejected from the nuclei; these are called α particles, β^- or β^+ particles, and γ rays. An α particle is a helium nucleus; a β^- particle is a high-speed electron and β^+ is the equivalent anti-particle called a "positron"; and γ rays are electromagnetic radiation, more energetic than x-rays. The original, radioactive atom is called the *parent* and the resulting more stable atom is called the *daughter*. The term *nuclide* is commonly used to describe any observable assemblage, no matter how unstable, of neutrons and protons in a nucleus. The radioactive decay rate of a collection of atoms of a particular unstable nuclide is proportional to the number of atoms present. The proportionality constant is called the decay constant, and the equation for radioactive decay can be written:

$\dfrac{dN}{dt}$ (incremental change of the number of atoms per incremental change in time) = rate of radioactivity decay = $-\lambda$(decay constant) $\times$ N(number of radioactive atoms present at that instant)

With time the number of radioactive atoms in the collection will be diminishing; since the decay constant itself does not vary for a particular nuclide, it is obvious that the rate of decay will also diminish with time. Hence the radioactivity of a collection of atoms at any time is a direct measure of the number of radioactive atoms remaining in the collection at the time sampled.

Figure 4–9 shows that radioactivity decreases *exponentially*, as is predicted by the mathematical solution of the equation we have written above. The *half-life* of a radioactive nuclide is the length of time it takes for the number to diminish by exactly half. It is related to the decay constant by the equation:

$$t_{1/2} \text{ (the half-life) } = 0.693/\lambda \text{ (the decay constant).}$$

The value 0.693 is simply the logarithm of 2 to the "natural base" (or base e), or 2.303 times the logarithm of 2 to the base ten.

It is evident that if the radioactive species undergoes decay to a radioactively stable daughter, a measure of the growth of the daughter will also be useful as a time indicator. It is this characteristic property of radioactivity, either the systematic decrease of the parent or the systematic increase of the daughter with time, that makes it useful as a geologic clock.

Three types of natural radioactivity have been used in the radioactive dating of geologic deposits (called "geochronometry"):

1. *Primary:* Nuclides of this type have half-lives so long that they are still present in measurable quantities approximately 5 billion years after the formation of the Solar System. These nuclides are potassium-40, rubidium-87, thorium-232, uranium-235, and uranium-238.

2. *Secondary:* The primary uranium isotopes and thorium-232 decay by a sequence of emission of α particles (doubly charged helium ions emitted by the nucleus), and β^- particles (fast-moving electrons proceeding from the nucleus). Intermediate radioactive daughters that are formed by these transformations have relatively short half-lives. Several of these nuclides, associated with the uranium decay series, whose half-lives are in the range of a hundred thousand years, have been used in geochronometry of deep-sea cores, namely thorium-230, protactinium-231, and uranium-234.

3. *Cosmic-ray induced:* Nuclides of this type, are being made continuously at the present time, principally by the action of cosmic rays. These are relatively short-lived nuclides which are sustained in the atmosphere and oceans at approximately constant levels by continuous production to make up for the loss by radioactive decay. Examples are: carbon-14, hydrogen-3, beryllium-7, beryllium-10, and silicon-32.

Before any of these radioactive nuclides can be used for measuring geologic time, however, certain conditions must be met: (1) The radioactive species which is used as the clock must be isolated from its daughter at the time of deposition, if the growth of the daughter is to be measured or, in a decay series, from its radioactive parent if the decay of the species is to be measured. (2) There must not be migration, in or out of the system, of the radioactive species used as the clock, or of the daughter if its growth is to be used. (3) The half-life of the radioactive nuclide must be suitable for the particular time range under study. It cannot be either too long or too short to be generally applicable.

All of the major types of natural radioactivity have been used in dating deposits on the deep ocean floor. We will proceed from methods used to date young deposits to methods that are used to date progressively older deposits. In so doing it will be evident that we will essentially be inverting the

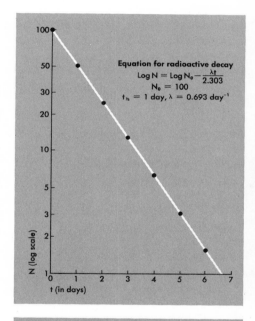

FIGURE 4–9 *Radioactive nuclides decay to more stable nuclides according to a definite law. This is called exponential decay as seen in the lower plot. N_0 is the number of original atoms (assumed 100 in this example) and N is the number of atoms left after a length of time t has elapsed. In the example the half-life, $t_{1/2}$, is chosen as one day, hence the decay constant, λ, is 0.693 day^{-1}. The upper curve is a plot of the logarithm of N against time. Exponential decay when plotted on semi-logarithmic coordinates, as was done here, results in a straight line. The conversion factor between natural logarithms and logarithms is given as ln (natural logarithm) $N = 2.303 \log N$, hence the slope of the line is*

$$\frac{-\lambda}{2.303} = -\log 2.$$

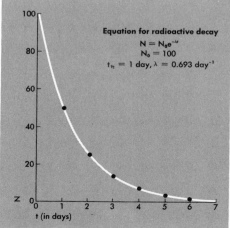

sequence of our listing of the natural forms of radioactivity. We will also highlight those methods which have been most generally useful.

Radiocarbon Dating

In 1946 Professor W. F. Libby discovered the natural occurrence of the isotope carbon-14. Since then it has been used for dating by archaeologists, anthropologists, geologists, and oceanographers.

Carbon-14 has a half life of 5,600 years, decaying to nitrogen-14 by the emission of a β^- particle. Before man began producing carbon-14 on a large scale by means of nuclear bombs, the principal agents of terrestrial production were cosmic rays interacting with the atmosphere. As cosmic ray particles (mainly protons traveling with energies measured in *billions* of electron volts) encounter the atmosphere, they interact with molecules to produce, among other products, fast-moving neutrons. These neutrons are slowed down through collisions with molecules in the atmosphere, and by the time they reach about 50,000 feet, they are very slow-moving; at this point they are called "thermal neutrons." Thermal neutrons react with nitrogen-14, which is the most abundant nuclide in the atmosphere, to produce carbon-14. The carbon-14 atoms combine with oxygen through a series of steps to form carbon dioxide, in which state it enters the carbon cycle on the Earth's surface.

Scientists have discovered that almost all the neutrons produced by cosmic rays are used up in the atmosphere to produce carbon-14, hence the easily measured production rate of neutrons approximates that of carbon-14; this has been determined to be about 9,800 grams of C^{14} per year for the whole Earth. Knowing the half-life of carbon-14 and the production rate, we can calculate the level of carbon-14 maintained at the Earth's surface. This value is 8.1×10^7 grams of carbon-14, or 8.29 grams per square centimeter of the Earth's surface. The distribution of carbon-14 in the various reservoirs (see Table 4–2) is roughly the same as the distribution of frequently cycled carbon (that is, carbon other than old fossil carbon in limestones and carbonaceous materials).

It is evident that the main reservoir—and therefore regulator—of carbon-14 is the ocean. Any material in contact with the sea, either directly or through carbon dioxide exchange via the atmosphere, will maintain a constant concentration of carbon-14 relative to the stable isotopes of carbon (carbon-12 and carbon-13).

Table 4–2

Distribution of Carbon-14

Reservoir on the Earth's Surface	Grams of C^{14} per cm^2 of Earth's Total Surface
Ocean (H_2CO_3, HCO_3^-, $CO_3^=$)	7.25
Organic carbon compounds in oceans (mainly dissolved)	0.59
Biosphere (living material)	0.33
Atmosphere (mainly CO_2)	0.12
Total	8.29

After Libby, 1955, *Radiocarbon Dating*, Wiley.

Stratigraphy and geochronometry of deep-sea deposits

64

Once carbon, in isotopic equilibrium with the major reservoir, is removed from exchange with the reservoir by an organism's death or the irreversible formation of plant cellulose or calcium carbonate shells, carbon-14 is no longer added to the system, and must decrease with time because of radioactive decay. By measuring the amount of carbon-14 relative to a stable carbon isotope (C^{12}) which does not alter in concentration with time, we can gauge how long the carbon-bearing material has been separated from the reservoir.

We have to assume that the abundance of carbon-14 relative to stable carbon has remained constant in the reservoir by the continuous production of carbon-14 by cosmic rays. The assumption of a constant ratio is reasonable for most dating purposes. But if at any time the cosmic ray flux had changed markedly or if carbon devoid of carbon-14 had been injected significantly into the reservoir (for instance, by the burning of coal and oil, the so-called fossil fuels), then the C^{14}/C^{12} ratio of the reservoir would have been altered. Such changes, small but measurable, have been noted.

The calcium carbonate tests and organic compounds found in deep-sea sediments can be dated by the carbon-14 method. By normal radioactive counting techniques it is possible to date samples as old as 40,000 years before the present. Radiocarbon dating of deep-sea cores has thus permitted us to measure the duration and end of the last major glacial period. The evidence is that the era of cold climate gave way to the present warmer conditions about 11,000 years ago. On the continents this change was marked by the retreat of the continental glaciers which covered large parts of Europe and North America. The oceans concurrently increased in volume—hence in depth—at a very rapid rate as the ice stored on the continents melted; at the same time the temperature of the surface waters increased.

The differences between glacial and post-glacial times were expressed in a variety of ways in the sedimentological record of parts of the deep sea. Some of these have already been discussed. One of the effects was the variation in accumulation rate of sediments in some parts of the oceans as a result of climatically controlled processes. In Fig. 4–10 we see a detailed analysis—by radiocarbon, paleontologic, and chemical methods—of a core raised in the equatorial mid-Atlantic. The core is rich in calcium carbonate, and the nonbiogenic component is mainly pelagic. The radical change in climate 11,000 years ago is tied to a sudden change in pelagic clay accumulation rate from 0.82 grams per square centimeter per thousand years during the glacial time to 0.22 grams per square centimeter per thousand years afterwards. The last major glacial event started 26,000 years ago, when the ice had retreated slightly on the continents.

Earlier we discussed the use of foraminiferan tests as climatic indicators of the Late Ice Age (or the Pleistocene Epoch). We have now seen that the most recent change from a glacial climate took place 11,000 years ago and was accompanied not only by biological changes in the oceans, but in places also by mineralogical changes (see Fig. 4–2) and changes in rates of accumulation. We can, thus, unambiguously assign a date of 11,000 years before the

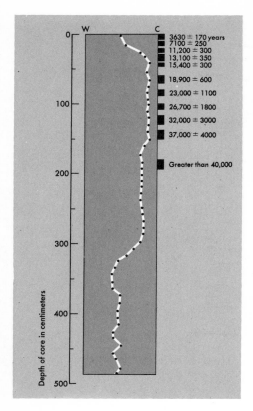

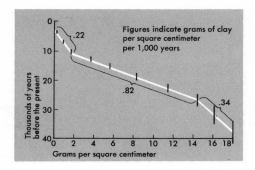

FIGURE 4-10 An analysis of an Atlantic equatorial core (A180-74) by radiocarbon dating, chemical and paleontologic methods. (Left) The climatic curve based on foraminiferan percentages as in Fig. 4-6 and radiocarbon dates at various levels in the core. (Right) A cumulative plot of calcium-carbonate-free sediment with time. Two breaks are noted. The younger, at 11,000 years before present, marks the end of the last major glacial period; the older, at 26,000 years, corresponds to the time of resurgence of glacial action resulting in the last major glacial period. The rate of clay accumulation is highest during glacial periods and lowest during the non-glacial period. (After Broecker, Turekian, and Heezen, 1958.)

present for this major event, whenever we find it by the stratigraphic techniques described above. When we know the composition of a deep-sea core down its length and an estimated time for the surface of the core (accounting for mixing by organisms and possible loss during recovery of the core), the additional time point at 11,000 years in the sediment column permits us to determine rates of accumulation of the various components for post-glacial time. We cannot extrapolate these rates to glacial times, however, because of the possibility, as we saw, of radical changes in rate as a function of the different sedimentologic patterns of glacial and nonglacial climates.

Figure 4-11 shows the distribution of post-glacial sediment accumulation rates of the nonbiogenic fraction in the Atlantic Ocean. It is evident that the nonbiogenic pelagic component accumulates slowly on the high spots and in areas remote from continents. The abyssal plains have higher accumulation rates generally, principally due to bottom-transported sediments.

Other Cosmic-Ray-Induced Nuclides Used in Dating

Two cosmic-ray-induced nuclides other than carbon-14—beryllium-10 and silicon-32—have been used in attempting to date deep-sea sediments. Unfortunately, neither is of general applicability and more work remains to be done

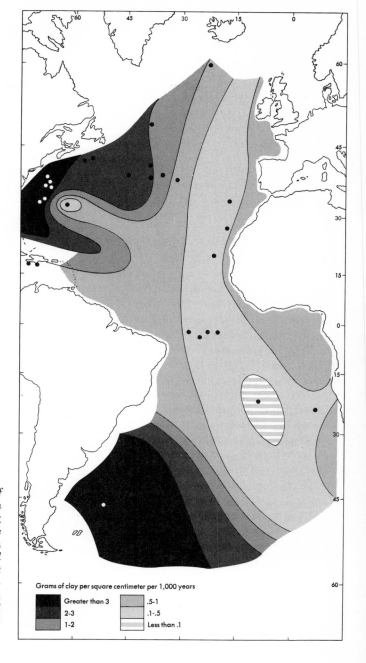

FIGURE 4–11 *Rates of deep-sea clay accumulation in the Atlantic Ocean during postglacial time. The rates are based on radiocarbon dates and paleontological correlations. The highest rates are in the western Atlantic basins, probably as a result of bottom-transported detritus. The lowest rates are along the topographic highs.*

Grams of clay per square centimeter per 1,000 years

Greater than 3	.5-1
2-3	.1-.5
1-2	Less than .1

on the methodology. Beryllium-10 has a half life of 2.5×10^6 years. If we assume a constant rate of deposition in a particular location, then the decay of Be^{10} can be followed down the length of a sediment core. Knowing the radioactivity of Be^{10} in the top of the core, we can get from the radioactivity at different depths in the core either a date for a particular point in the core or a rate of accumulation if comparisons are made between different levels in the core. Silicon-32 has a half-life of about 500 years. If at the time of deposition the amount of Si^{32} relative to ordinary silicon incorporated in the tests of siliceous organisms (such as diatoms, sponge spicules, and radiolarians) is assumed to be constant, as with carbon-14, then the decay of silcon-32 can be followed down the core for information on absolute ages or rates of accumulation. The technique is applicable only in areas of rapid silica accumulation, as in the diatomaceous sediments of the Antarctic Ocean.

Uranium Decay Series

Normally, piston-coring, with a maximum penetration of 20 meters, can reach through continuous, undisturbed deep-sea sediments to sample into the Pleistocene Epoch. As we have seen for cores rich in calcium carbonate, from the evidence of paleontology or of oxygen isotopes that is a function of water temperature, we can attempt to relate events recorded in the deep-sea sediments to terrestrial events influenced by glacial activity of the Ice Age. Because of the practical limit of radiocarbon dating, these correlations are tenuous beyond 40,000 years, which takes in only the last major glacial period. For dating the last few hundred thousand years in deep-sea sediments and some other types of marine deposits, the main effort has been centered in the uranium decay series.

The two isotopes of uranium, U^{238} and U^{235}, decay stepwise by the emission of alpha and beta particles (with associated gamma rays) to the stable end products of lead, Pb^{206} and Pb^{207}, respectively. Some of the daughter nuclides near the beginning of the decay scheme can be used in the dating of marine deposits because of their distinctive chemistries and suitable half-lives. The following are the decay schemes for the uranium isotopes showing, underlined, the daughters that have been used in dating.

$$(1)\ U^{238} \xrightarrow{4.49 \times 10^9 y} Th^{234} \xrightarrow{24.1d} Pa^{234} \xrightarrow{1.18m} U^{234} \xrightarrow{2.48 \times 10^5 y}$$

$$\underline{Th^{230}} \xrightarrow{7.5 \times 10^4 y} Ra^{226} \xrightarrow{1622y} Rn^{222} \xrightarrow{3.825d} \text{stepwise down to stable } Pb^{206}$$

$$(2)\ U^{235} \xrightarrow{7.13 \times 10^8 y} Th^{231} \xrightarrow{25.6h} \underline{Pa^{231}} \xrightarrow{3.43 \times 10^4 y} \text{stepwise down to stable } Pb^{207}$$

In the dating of deep-sea sediments, the two most important nuclides are Th^{230}, which has a half-life of 75,000 years, and Pa^{231}, which has a half-life of 34,300 years. The basic chemical properties of these two nuclides are very similar to each other and radically different from those of uranium. This can be seen most clearly by comparing the geochemistries of uranium and the very long-lived isotope of thorium, Th^{232}, which has its own decay series. In rocks the ratio of Th^{232} to U^{238} is about four, but this is strongly altered in sea water. The oceans are slightly basic and contain dissolved carbonate and bicarbonate ions, as was implied in the section on carbon-14 dating. In such a solution, thorium is highly insoluble as a phosphate while uranium forms strong bonds with the carbonate ions, resulting in a highly soluble complex. The concentration of uranium in sea water is thus three micrograms (10^{-6} grams) per liter and that of thorium (Th^{232}) is less than 0.0015 micrograms per liter. The ratio of Th^{232} to U^{238} then becomes 0.0005 compared to the ratio in rock of *four*.

Since the isotopes of an element all have the same chemical properties, to a very good first approximation, the fate of Th^{230} and the chemically similar Pa^{231} produced in sea water by the radioactive decay of uranium is predicted by the observed behavior of Th^{232}: Th^{230} and Pa^{231} will be removed rapidly from sea water as insoluble phases and deposited on the ocean floor. Hence, these nuclides will be found in deep-sea sediments in excess amounts above that expected in radioactive equilibrium with uranium found in detritus derived from land. There will, however, be no excess of uranium in most deep-sea sediments because of its high solubility dut to soluble complex formation with carbonate.

If the excess Th^{230} or excess Pa^{231} accumulates on the deep-sea floor at a constant rate associated with particles that are also accumulating at a constant rate, it is possible to determine the age at any depth in the core by comparing the Th^{230} or Pa^{231} radioactivity at that level with the radioactivity at the top of the core, knowing the half-lives of the nuclides. Alternatively the rate of accumulation can be determined by measuring the rate of decrease of Th^{230} or Pa^{231} radioactivity with depth (Fig. 4–12).

Comparisons between the uranium-decay-series techniques and the radiocarbon technique indicate that the degree of correspondence may vary depending on location. Generally, cores from the Atlantic Ocean show poor correlation of rates of accumulation between those determined by the Th^{230}

FIGURE 4–12 *A plot of the excess Th^{230} (i.e., unsupported by the uranium in the core) with depth in a Caribbean core (V12–122). The semi-logarithmic plot indicates that a straight line can be drawn through all the points (the white line). This corresponds to a total accumulation rate for this high-calcium-carbonate core of 2.8 cm/1,000y. The lettered zones are indications of worldwide climate: Z, X, V are warm times; Y, W, U are glacial times. (After Ku and Broecker, 1966.)*

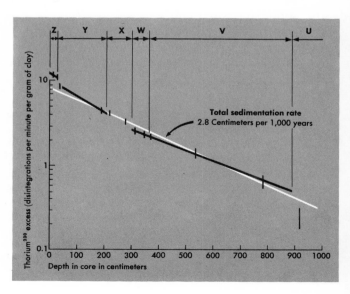

or Pa[231] methods and the carbon-14 method. This can be ascribed to the fact that clay accumulation rates and clay mineral proportions can vary greatly in the Atlantic Ocean because of the close proximity to continental sources of sediments. Where there are no radical changes in accumulation rates or clay mineral proportions with time, as in the Pacific, and Indian Oceans and parts of the Caribbean, the uranium-decay-series methods probably give reasonable dates and rates of accumulation and agree with those based on carbon-14.

The generalized, dated climatic sequence back through 300,000 years as inferred from deep-sea cores through the use of these techniques is shown in Figure 4–13.

We can also make direct correlation with world-wide events as seen on land for some of the events of the last several hundred thousand years. At the present time sea level is about 100 meters higher than during the most recent peak of glaciation 18,000 years ago. Yet there remains a large storehouse of water in the glacial ice of Antarctica and Greenland. If all of this were to melt, sea level would rise another 30 meters. There is evidence that in the interglacial period which ended 120,000 years ago sea level was higher by about 3 meters. This evidence lies in the existence of raised coral benches that grew in place, when alive, just at sea level at low tide. The aragonitic corals have a high uranium concentration (about three parts per million) and incorporate essentially no thorium isotopes at the time of formation. The uranium decay series thus can be used to date corals by measuring the growth of Th[230] by the decay of uranium. Thus, a clear relation between climate, sea level, and events along the shore lines of islands and continents can be related by means of radioactive dating of both shallow water and deep ocean deposits with the uranium decay series.

Despite these marked successes in dating and correlation, the maximum extent of the utility of the uranium decay series is 300,000 years. Hence, although our uranium dating range is ten times the radiocarbon range, we are still a long way from being able to detail the older events of the Pleistocene Epoch and of earlier times.

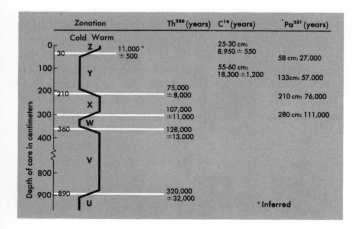

FIGURE 4–13 *Ages by a variety of methods on core V12–122 (see Fig. 4–12). There is reasonably good correlation of these independent ages. The 11,000-year age is inferred from other cores. (After Ku and Broecker, 1966.)*

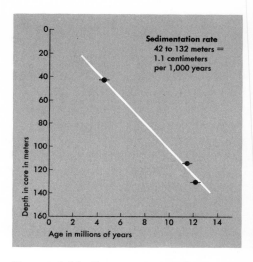

FIGURE 4–14 *Potassium-argon dates on glass layers in the core drilled off Guadelupe Island as an experiment in deep-water drilling. In other cores volcanic minerals such as biotite mica and feldspars have been used to obtain dates. (After Dymond, 1966.)*

Methods of Dating Older Material in Deep-sea Cores

There are two ways of dating beyond the 300,000-year limit of the uranium decay series. Both are based ultimately on the potassium-argon method. One isotope of potassium, K^{40}, is radioactive with a half-life of 12.4×10^9 years. Of the decay products 88 per cent is Ca^{40}, which is the common isotope of calcium, and 12 per cent is Ar^{40}, a rare gas. The argon, trapped in the lattice of potassium-bearing rocks and minerals, accumulates if the temperature of the material is kept below $300°C$. By measuring the potassium-argon ratio in a rock or mineral, we can measure geologic time. This method, because of its extreme sensitivity, can be used to date materials as young as several hundred thousand years and as old as the age of the Earth.

We cannot date the major part of nonbiogenic deep-sea sediments by this method although they are high in potassium concentration, because the detrital clay minerals of the deep-sea sediments contain relict argon derived from weathered continental material. Recently deposited sediments in the deep-sea for instance give "ages" of 200 to 400 million years in the Atlantic Ocean and about 80 million years in the Pacific because the argon was not lost during weathering.

Associated with deep-sea detrital sediments, however, are volcanic layers. Potassium-argon dates *can* be obtained on these materials because when they were molten all the argon was lost, and any argon measured now had to have formed as the result of the potassium-40 decay. Figure 4–14 shows the analysis of a 500-foot core obtained in the preliminary deep-sea Mohole drilling experiment off Guadelupe Island. The rates of accumulation are compatible with rates obtained by the uranium-decay-series in the Pacific Ocean.

The second method of using potassium-argon dating is less direct. As discussed above, the polarity of the magnetic field has changed during the Earth's history. This change from the present-day "normal" polarity to a "reversed" polarity, and so back and forth, influences the magnetic orientation of iron-bearing minerals susceptible to magnetization. Since these minerals occur both in a cooling lava on land and in slowly settling particles at sea, correlation between events on land and sea are possible. As discussed earlier in this chapter the potassium-argon dating of volcanic rocks on the Hawaiian Islands and elsewhere gives a record of the magnetic field reversals (see Fig. 4–5). These may be traced in deep-sea cores and the related ages assigned to each core level (Fig. 4–15). As already mentioned this technique is most successful in cores raised at high latitudes. Further correlation to deep-sea cores raised from the ocean bottom at lower latitudes must be achieved primarily with paleontologic data such as the appearance or disappearance of species.

Table 4–3 summarizes the dating techniques used in the study of deep-sea sediments and their effective ranges of application.

Table 4–3

Dating Techniques
for Deep-sea Sediments

Nuclide	Range (years)
Carbon-14	0 to 40,000
Protactinium-231	0 to 150,000
Thorium-230	0 to 300,000
Potassium-40/argon-40 (in volcanic material)	∼100,000 and older
Potassium-40/argon-40 (dating on land of magnetic reversals and correlation of these reversals with those found in deep-sea cores)	700,000 to 4,500,000

FIGURE 4–15 *Magnetic stratigraphy used in dating deep-sea cores and stratigraphic correlation. Normally and reversely magnetized levels can be correlated over the Antarctic area and can be compared with radiolarian faunal zones (shown by Greek letters). (After Opdyke, Glass, Hays, and Foster, 1966.)*

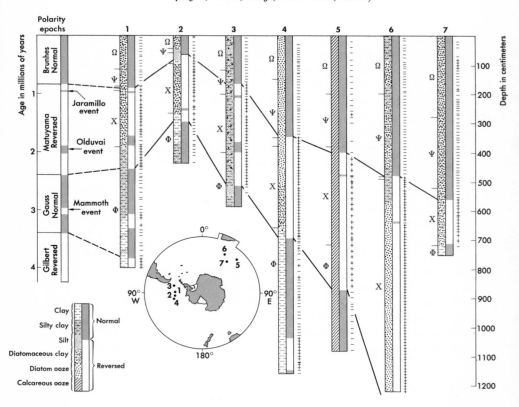

5

The oceans in motion

Up to this point we have considered in detail the ocean basins and their sediments, taking for granted the existence of the ocean water filling the basins. Yet the properties of the ocean water itself are of fundamental importance in understanding the surface history of the Earth.

To the most ancient human communities bordering the seas, these properties gradually became familiar as the oceans were exploited for food and travel. Knowledge of its saltiness and biological productivity, of the variations of roughness and temperature due to climate, and of the currents and tides—all this became part of the cultures of seafaring communities such as the Phoenicians, the Polynesians, and the Vikings. The legacy of these ancient mariners, refined by the experience of our most recent European and Asian sea-going ancestors, has provided the framework for our modern study of the seas. The properties of ocean water that have been of perennial interest to mankind continue to be of fundamental concern today. Only now the chemical and physical properties and the patterns and periodicities of the ocean are studied with highly sensitive instruments on a world-wide scale and the results are placed in the context of the laws of physics. By these methods we understand the oceans in motion, that is, the nature of tides, currents and large-scale ocean mixing.

Chemical and Physical Properties of Ocean Water

We can use the variations of the chemical and physical properties of ocean water to define its large-scale motions if we can identify the sources of these variations. To do so it is necessary to sample the oceans in depth as well as breadth.

It is not a difficult matter to sample the surface of the ocean for chemical or physical analysis. One can dip a bucket or use a pump and hose and have all the water necessary for making the desired chemical or physical measurements. But it is a little harder to obtain a sample of water from the ocean deeps with accurate measures of depth and temperature and with assurance that the sample is unmixed with surrounding waters. One effective solution to this problem is seen in the Nansen bottle for sampling ocean water and ocean temperature at great depths (Fig. 5–1). The bottles are spaced along a wire as it is let out from a ship by means of a metered winch (a device used to raise and lower cables aboard the ship). Hence, the depth of each bottle on the wire can be approximately determined. A more precise depth is obtained by measuring the amount of compression of a mercury thermometer in direct contact with sea water. The increasing pressure of the water with depth produces a different reading from that of a protected thermometer. Thus, both temperature and depth can be measured with these two thermometers attached to the bottle. Each Nansen bottle, or comparable container, samples about one to two liters of sea water.

Information on the temperature distribution with depth can also be obtained by means of thermisters (thermocouples, sensitive to temperature) attached to a sediment-coring tube.

Composition

If you were to sample the ocean all over the world with the above techniques and to use the most accurate methods of chemical analysis for determining the composition of the sea water at each location, you would find that, although the total amount of dissolved salts is variable, the relative proportions of the major elements (Na, Cl, Mg, Ca, etc.) are constant. This fact was ascertained by successively more accurate analyses by chemists throughout the nineteenth century, culminating in the definitive study by W. Dittmar on water samples collected on the *Challenger* expedition in the 1870's.

The saltiness of the ocean, or *salinity,* is defined as the number of grams

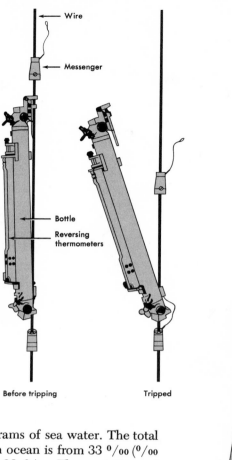

FIGURE 5-1 *Sampling sea water and temperature at depth using a Nansen bottle. The diagram shows the bottle being released by a messenger (commonly made of lead) sliding down the wire. As the messenger hits the bottle, the latter is released, resulting in the trapping of the water and the freezing-in of the mercury thermometer readings. Another lead messenger is also released that trips the next bottle down the wire and so on. (H. O. Pub. No. 607, U.S. Naval Oceanographic Office 1955.)*

of dissolved salts in 1,000 grams of sea water. The total range of salinity of the open ocean is from 33 $^0/_{00}$ ($^0/_{00}$ = parts per thousand) to 38 $^0/_{00}$. The variations of salinity in the open ocean are the result of a number of competing processes: concentration effects, such as evaporation and ice-flow formation; and dilution effects, such as atmospheric precipitation, stream run-off, and melting ice. Nearshore waters range both down to even lower salinities because of dilution by fresh water from streams and up to higher salinities because of intense evaporation in arid climates.

The average concentration of the main components of sea water with a salinity of 35 $^0/_{00}$ is shown in Table 5-1. Because of the constancy of the different elements relative to each other in sea water, it is evident that the measure of the concentration of any one element in a sea water sample would be an index of the salinity. It has been common practice to determine salinity by measuring the amount of chloride by chemical means and applying the equation:

$$\text{salinity} = 0.03 + 1.805 \times \text{chlorinity}$$
(chlorinity = grams of chloride in 1,000 grams of sea water)

The oceans in motion

Conductometric measurements of salinity are now commonly made. This type of measurement depends on the fact that a salt solution will conduct an electric current. At a given temperature the higher the salinity the greater the conductivity measured.

Temperature

We can think of the oceans as a gigantic pump which transfers heat from the equator to the poles. Heat from the sun is pumped from low latitudes to high latitudes, where it is released to the atmosphere. This transfer is effected in the surface waters of the ocean by strong currents such as the Gulf Stream moving warm tropical waters to polar regions. The deep waters of the oceans (by which we mean water below a depth of about 1,500 meters) all have their origins in the high latitudes, as we shall see. Hence, the deep waters of the oceans are considerably colder than the surface waters.

Figure 5–2 is a typical profile showing the temperature stratification in the oceans. The main features of this profile are: (1) a surface, or *mixed*, layer reflecting the temperature of the ambiant average temperature of that latitude, (2) a deep (and bottom) layer reflecting the origin of the water in high latitudes, and (3) a *thermocline* layer between about 100 meters and 1,500 meters in which the temperature generally decreases monotonically from the high surface value to the low deep value.

The thermocline layer indicates that there is transfer of heat vertically from the surface waters to the deep waters as well as horizontally. Although some of this transfer occurs by molecular heat diffusion, much of it is accomplished by small eddy currents which transport water vertically, thus mixing salinities as well as temperatures.

Table 5–1

Concentrations of the Major Components of Sea Water*

Component	Grams per Kilogram
Chloride	19.353
Sodium	10.76
Sulfate	2.712
Magnesium	1.294
Calcium	0.413
Potassium	0.387
Bicarbonate	0.142
Bromide	0.067
Strontium	0.008
Boron	0.004
Fluoride	0.001

Culkin, 1965 in *Chemical Oceanography*, ed. by Riley and Skirrow.

*For a salinity of 35 °/oo.

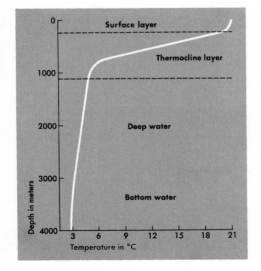

FIGURE 5–2 *The general vertical thermal structure of the ocean. (After von Arx, 1962.)*

Density

The density of sea water is a function of temperature and salinity. The higher the temperature, the lower the density for a given salinity; and the higher the salinity, the higher the density for a given temperature. Figure 5–3 is a plot of salinity against temperature. Lines connecting points of equal-density waters are called *isopycnal* lines. It is evident that cold, highly saline water is denser than warm, low salinity water. As with all fluids, any variation of density in parts of the fluid will cause a redistribution so that a density stratification is effected. This is clearly seen when immiscible oil floats on water because of the oil's lower density. Although ocean water of one density is com-

FIGURE 5–3   *The relation between temperature and salinity below 200 meters for the Atlantic, Pacific, and Indian Oceans. The symbol σ_t represents the density minus one times 1,000 at the one atmosphere pressure. A sea water density of 1.0280 thus has a $\sigma_t = 28.0$. The high-temperature—high-salinity region is the water at about 200 meters. The areas represent data for each total ocean system. There are distinctive water masses defined within each ocean as well. Note the effect of high salinity water types injected into the Atlantic Ocean (Mediterranean water) and the Indian Ocean (Red Sea water). Antarctic Bottom Water, common to all the oceans, is the densest of all water masses. (After Dietrich, 1963.)*

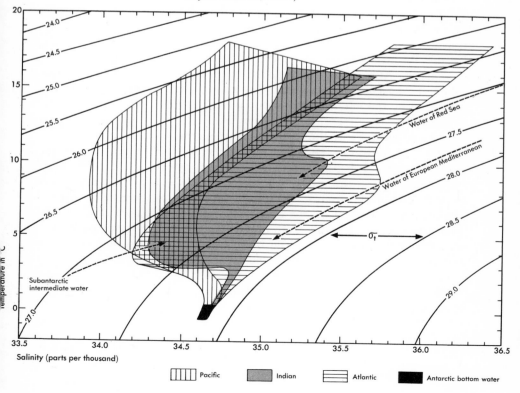

pletely miscible with ocean water of another density, the process of mixing takes a long time, since it depends on diffusion and convective mixing; hence waters of different density tend to be stratified.

Oceanic Circulation

It is the heat of the sun that ultimately is responsible for the circulation of the oceans. The oceans circulate in response to two distinct expressions of the interaction of solar energy with the surface of the Earth: (1) The winds, generated in the atmosphere by differential heating, couple with the surface layers of the ocean to produce a wind-driven circulation system. (2) Evaporation and chilling produce variations in density that cause readjustments to the Earth's gravity field by the movement of water masses; this movement drives the deep circulation of the oceans and is called a thermohaline circulation system. We will briefly describe the main features of each system.

Surface Currents: The Wind-driven Circulation System

Figure 2–8 is a chart of the surface currents of the oceans. It is evident that the major features in the Atlantic and Pacific Oceans are large circular patterns of currents ("gyres"), clockwise in the northern hemisphere and counterclockwise in the southern. These observed patterns are the result, primarily, of the response of the ocean surface to the major wind patterns. On either side of the equator the winds move, in general, from east to west; they are called the *trade winds*. At about 40° latitude the winds move from west to east and are called the *prevailing westerlies*. The atmospheric circulation patterns are controlled by the movement of air on a rotating Earth. The rotation also has a direct effect on the oceans, but the indirect effect by means of wind is most responsible for defining the surface current patterns.

The Gulf Stream in the North Atlantic is perhaps the most famous of the surface currents. It is part of the clockwise gyre system of the North Atlantic. Originating in the eastern end of the Gulf of Mexico, it moves northward through the Florida Straits hugging the continental margin as far as Cape Hatteras, it then turns toward the open ocean and, farther north and east it becomes the North Atlantic Current (or "Drift") that is responsible for the warming of the British Isles. The Gulf Stream marks the boundary of warm surface water to the south and cold surface water from the north. At this boundary a strong narrow current develops that results in the transfer of warm water northward. It is to be noted that the Gulf Stream is not a current of warm water flowing *through* cold water.

Along the western coasts of continents, surface water is transported away from the continent by wind action, resulting in the upwelling of deeper waters (down to depths of about 300 meters). Areas of upwelling are marked at the surface by high biological productivity because of the continuous supply of nutrient elements such as phosphorus that are brought to the surface. Any change in the intensity of winds affects the rate of upwelling, resulting in dramatic changes in biological productivity.

The Deep Circulation of the Oceans: Thermohaline Circulation

In deep circulation the controlling factor is density stratification in the Earth's gravity field. It is a common experience to see the denser of two fluids placed in a container sink to the bottom—the separation of oil and water, for example. Water may become denser with increased salinity, decreased temperature, or both, hence circulation based on these factors is called thermohaline. The distinctive temperature and salinity attained by a body of water as a result of chilling, evaporation, freezing, dilution by rain or meltwater, or a combination of these processes will designate it as a *water type*. Once a water type is formed, it seeks its level in the ocean based on its density; and as it does, it displaces surrounding water. Since a water type is produced continuously from year to year, the oceans must keep circulating to accommodate the continuously supplied waters. Temperature and salinity changes take place by mixing with adjacent water types; in addition, temperature may be raised in part by heating from the Earth's interior through the bottom of the ocean.

In a temperature-salinity curve the mixing of one water type with another is represented by a continuous trend which can be used to identify the major *water masses* of the oceans (Fig. 5–3). Hence, a distinctive water mass is the mixture of two (or possibly more) water types with a definable range of salinities and temperatures. Since water masses are more easily defined by oceanographic techniques than water types are, the deep circulation of the oceans is expressed in terms of water masses. The oceanic structure of the Atlantic Ocean has been studied intensively by identifying water masses through temperature-salinity data. The results are shown in Fig. 5–4. For an idea of the origin of various water masses, consider the following examples:

North Atlantic Deep Water (NADW) is believed to form when warm Gulf Stream water, which is highly saline as the result of evaporation in the low latitudes, is chilled by mixing with cold, less saline Arctic water near Greenland. The resulting dense water sinks to the bottom of the North Atlantic Basin. From there it can be traced southward until, before it is obscured by mixing, it approaches the surface in the Antarctic region.

Antarctic Bottom Water (AABW) is formed in the following way. Water in the Weddell sea is chilled in the Antarctic winter so that relatively salt-free sea-ice is formed, leaving a cold, very saline brine. This descends to the ocean bottom mixing on the way down with less saline water. The mixing decreases

The oceans in motion

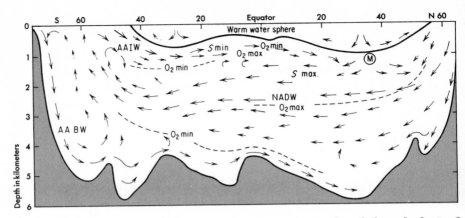

FIGURE 5-4 *The major water masses of the Atlantic Ocean identified on the basis of salinity-temperature plots similar to those in Fig. 5–3. The arrows show the main directions of water flow. AAIW is Antarctic Intermediate Water and* Ⓜ *is Mediterranean water (flowing from east to west). The maximum and minimum oxygen concentrations are also shown as they help to identify water masses. "S min" and "S max" are the salinity minimum and maximum layers in the deep ocean.*

its saltiness but not its temperature. What results is the densest water in all the oceans, water which occupies the bottom position. In the Atlantic Ocean it can be traced along the bottom as far as 20°N, at which point the North Atlantic Deep Water rides over it on its southward journey.

The other water masses of Fig. 5–4 are formed in somewhat similar ways and occupy the levels dictated by their densities. All the water masses are the result of mixing of water types. The farther from the source of the water type the greater the amount of mixing with surrounding waters, until ultimately homogenization as the result of diffusion occurs; at this point the identity of the water mass is lost.

Oceanic Mixing Rates

We have been able to identify the major water masses of the oceans primarily by measuring the distribution of salinity and temperature with geography and depth. It is evident that this structure of the oceans can be maintained only if there is a continuous supply of each water type to give continuing definition to the water masses, which would otherwise be lost by random mixing processes. Hence, the deep oceans circulate as well as the surface currents although at much slower rates. With the help of radioactive tracers we can try to guess at the rates of deep ocean circulation. There are two ways of expressing our knowledge of circulation rates in the oceans: We can follow a particular water mass from its source (that is, where the defining water type is formed) as it flows by displacement in the deep ocean basins. Alternatively we can divide all the ocean basins into a group of interconnected reservoirs and ask the question, how long do water molecules remain in each reservoir? Both methods have been used.

The method of following a water mass "downstream" can be demonstrated by an example from the Pacific Ocean. In the Pacific as in the Atlantic, as was implied above, the bottom water is derived from the Antarctic region. Since there is no other source of dense water in the North Pacific as there is in the North Atlantic, the movement of water in the Pacific Ocean can be resolved essentially into northward-flowing bottom water below 2,500 meters and a southward return above 2,500 meters. If we had a timing device moving with the bottom water, we could estimate the rate of movement of this water mass and thus the rate of stirring in the Pacific Ocean.

Such a timing device is available in dissolved carbon-14. Figure 5–5 shows the relative carbon-14 ages of Pacific Deep Water as a function of latitude. It is evident that although the water mass originates in the Antarctic, the carbonate ($CO_3^=$) and bicarbonate (HCO_3^-) species in the water did not have time to equilibrate completely with the atmosphere, hence giving formal ages of greater than 600 years.

As the bottom water moves northward, pushed by the continually formed water mass in the Antarctic, the carbon-14 abundance inherited from the Antarctic region decays radioactively. Since no new carbon-14 is injected along the way, a measure of the decrease in carbon-14 can be used to measure time elapsed by movement of the bottom water from latitude to latitude in just the same manner as carbon-14 is used to date deep-sea sediment cores. Knowing the difference in time shown by the water mass from one latitude to

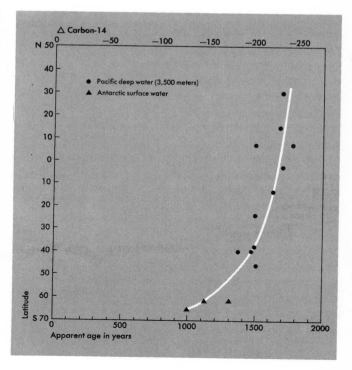

FIGURE 5–5 *Carbon-14 values for Pacific Ocean deep waters and Antarctic Ocean surface waters. ΔC^{14} is a measure of the C^{14}/C^{12} ratio relative to the value expected in sea water completely equilibrated with modern atmospheric carbon-14. Negative values mean that the carbon-14 is decreasing because of radioactive decay. The amount of decrease can be related to elapsed time because of the known half-life of carbon-14. This figure indicates that Pacific Deep Water originates in the Antarctic and flows northward at a rate of 0.05 cm/sec. (Data from Bien, Rakestraw, and Seuss of the Scripps Institution of Oceanography; analyzed by Knauss, 1962.)*

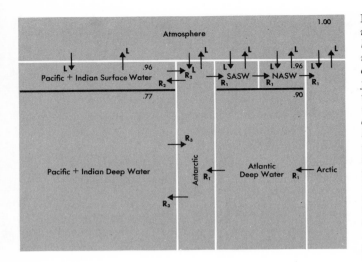

FIGURE 5–6 *Typical box-model used in evaluating large-scale ocean mixing rates. Arrows represent the direction of mixing inferred from oceanographic measurements. L is the specific rate of transfer of carbon across the ocean-atmosphere boundary; R stands for the rate of transport of carbon between oceanic reservoirs represented by the boxes. The total amount of carbon in each box is known and the numbers indicate the relative amounts of carbon-14 to carbon-12 as compared to an atmospheric value of 1.00. The mean residence times in years of carbon and associated water in each reservoir from this analysis are: Arctic-45; NASW (North Atlantic Surface Water) 10; SASW (South Atlantic Surface Water)-10; Atlantic Deep Water-600; Antarctic-100; Pacific + Indian Surface Water-25; Pacific + Indian Deep Water-1300. Other models give similar results. (After Broecker, Gerard, Ewing, and Heezen, 1961, in Oceanography, ed. by Sears.)*

the next along its path, and knowing the size of the water mass, we can arrive at an average velocity of transport and a rate of water transport northward in the Pacific along the bottom. As this water must return, such a calculation gives us a good idea of the rate of mixing of the Pacific Ocean.

The total transit time from 60°S to 30°N is less than 600 years. An analysis of the data indicates that at the equator, where the cross section of Pacific Deep Water is $28 \times 10^9 m^2$, the Pacific Deep Water has an average velocity of 0.05 cm/sec or a total flux of $14 \times 10^6 m^3$ sec.

The other method of describing the rates of mixing in the oceans involves dividing the ocean into a series of interconnected reservoirs. At the ocean surface there is an exchange of carbon between the ocean and the atmosphere, but the rate of mixing of the oceans is not rapid enough to result in equilibration of the total atmospheric and oceanic reservoirs as far as carbon-14 is concerned. The resulting variation of the carbon-14 content of different parts of the oceans can be analyzed in terms of *mean residence times* of dissolved carbon and the associated water in each defined reservoir.

One model is shown in Fig. 5–6. It can be seen that the mean residence time of a molecule of carbon (hence of associated water) is greatest for the deep Pacific Ocean.

Tides and Waves

In addition to the circulation of the oceans, there are other types of motions of the sea more common to everyday experience. There are the periodic motions we call tides and waves. The major tidal cycles, by which we mean the periodic rising and falling of the sea as seen by gauges along the coast, are astronomical in origin with the Moon playing the main role. Waves are produced by the action of winds on surface waters. They share the common property that they represent periodic motions in the oceans.

Tides

Newton's law of gravity describes the force exerted in a system as a result of gravitational attraction. This is written:

$$F = \frac{Gm_1 m_2}{r^2}$$

where: F = force

G = universal gravitational constant

m_1 and m_2 = the masses of the two bodies

r = the distance between the centers of mass of the two bodies.

Newton's law also predicts that two bodies will formally rotate around a common center of gravity if their centrifugal force just equals the attractive force. Although the Moon visually appears to revolve around the Earth actually there is an almost invisible motion of the Earth around the Moon as well. The axis of rotation of the Earth-Moon system is actually 1,700 kilometers below the surface of the Earth rather than at its center (6,373 kilometers down).

This rotation produces a centrifugal force at all points of the Earth. This is a different and lesser centrifugal force than is exerted by the Earth rotating on its axis, but it is involved nevertheless in determining the net tide-producing forces on the Earth. The Earth-Moon system as a whole is balanced with respect to both the attractive and the centrifugal forces, but individual elements on the two bodies respond to the resultant force acting at that point. At any point on the Earth the resultant of the two forces associated with the Moon-Earth system will be operative—the force of attraction and the centrifugal force (Fig. 5–7). This resultant force varies at each geographic point as the moon revolves around the Earth and tends to move the Earth's surface out of shape to adjust to its presence. The Earth, despite its rigidity, does respond to a small degree to this force, producing Earth tides. The main effect, however, is in the oceans.

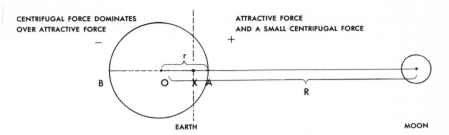

R = distance between center of Earth and center of Moon = 384,000 km
r = radius of the Earth = 6400 km
X = center of mass of Earth-Moon system
x = distance X-A = 1700 km
G = universal gravitational constant = 6.7×10^{-8} dynes cm²g^{-2}
M = mass of Moon = 7.4×10^{25} grams
T = period of Moon's revolution around Earth = 27 days

	ATTRACTIVE FORCE	CENTRIFUGAL FORCE
Sublunar point (A) (unit mass)	$\dfrac{GM}{(R-r)^2}$	$\dfrac{x\,4\pi^2}{T^2}$
Opposite side (B) (unit mass)	$\dfrac{GM}{(R+r)^2}$	$-\dfrac{(2r-x)\,4\pi^2}{T^2}$

NET TIDE-PRODUCING FORCE ON A UNIT MASS

Sublunar point A $\qquad \dfrac{GM}{(R-r)^2} + \dfrac{x\,4\pi^2}{T^2}$

$\qquad\qquad\qquad\qquad$ 3.4 $\quad$ + 1.2 $\quad$ = 4.6×10^{-3} dynes

Opposite point B $\qquad \dfrac{GM}{(R+r)^2} - \dfrac{(2r-x)\,4\pi^2}{T^2}$

$\qquad\qquad\qquad\qquad$ 3.2 $\quad$ − 7.8 $\quad$ = -4.6×10^{-3} dynes

FIGURE 5–7 *An idealized representation of the tide-producing force of the Moon. The Earth-Moon system rotates around an axis that intersects a line drawn between the centers of the Earth and Moon at 1,700 kilometers below the Earth's surface on the side facing the Moon. The tide-producing force on a mass of water is a very small fraction of the attractive force of the Earth on that mass of water.*

Under our simple model of lunar attraction the oceans tend to move towards the sublunar point and at a point on the diametrically opposite side as shown in Fig. 5–7. A particular point on the Earth's surface will experience, in one day, two high tides and two low tides. This is called a semi-diurnal tidal cycle. Because the solar day is 24 hours while 24 hours and 50 minutes pass before the Moon is again over the same spot on the Earth, because of the Moon's revolution around the Earth, the beginning of a particular cycle at a point on the Earth will be offset 50 minutes each day from the previous day.

The oceans in motion

In addition to the dominant effect of the Moon, the Sun also exerts a strong tidal effect on the Earth (about 46 per cent of the Moon's force). Since the plane of the Moon's orbit around the Earth is not exactly in the same plane as the Earth's orbit around the Sun, there are complex effects on the tidal cycles generated by the action of the two forces. Hence, in different parts of the Earth one can find mixtures of semi-diurnal and full diurnal tidal cycles, depending on the lunar and solar effects. These are seen in Fig. 5–8 which compares tidal gauge records for several different locations on the world ocean.

It is evident that when the Earth, Moon, and Sun are lined up (or as astronomers say in "opposition" or "conjunction"), the tidal range for semi-diurnal areas will be maximum because of the combined effects of the two astronomic bodies on the Earth. These occur a few days after the full ("opposi-

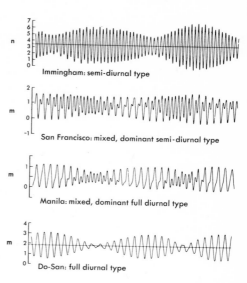

FIGURE 5–8 *Tidal patterns during March, 1936, at Immingham, England; San Francisco, California; Manila, Philippines; and Do San, Vietnam. The patterns differ because of the differing relative effects of the forces exerted by the Sun and Moon at the various locations on the Earth. (After Defant, 1961.)*

tion" as used above) and new ("conjunction") moons and are called *spring tides*.

Since the tides are periodic phenomena, in a fluid they are sensitive to the boundaries of the container—the configuration of the oceans, bays, sounds, inlets, and so on. For this reason, at a particular location the tidal cycle may be very complex. A great deal of study has gone into constructing tide tables for seaports all over the world to predict the tidal sequences and ranges.

Waves

Waves can be generated in a body of water such as a swimming pool or a lake by one of two methods. You can drop a pebble in the water and see a concentric wave pattern develop and spread away from the point of impact, or you can blow air over the surface of the water by means of an electric fan or other device. Similar processes are involved in making waves in the oceans. The analog to dropping a pebble in the water is the transmission of energy to the ocean by an earthquake, volcanic explosion, or landslide on the ocean's margins and floors. Such a wave is called a *tsunami* and travels at a velocity of about 500 miles per hour. These are relatively rare events compared to the continuous wave generation by winds, but they are nevertheless quite spectacular and destructive when they encounter coasts.

The oceans in motion

By far the most common waves in the oceans are those generated by winds. When a wind blows over the surface of the oceans it piles up the water in ridges whose height and periodicity reflect the intensity of the wind. If the oceans were initially glassy smooth and flat, a sustained wind of constant strength and direction would produce a clearly discernible rippled effect observable for great distances away from the point of generation. As the waves move away from the source, the smaller waves are eliminated in favor of the long-period wave, resulting in a pronounced *swell*. The swells move with velocities that are related to their wavelengths, as seen in Table 5–2. Of course, the interaction of winds with the ocean varies in both direction and intensity, resulting in a complex pattern called a "sea" (Fig. 5–9). In principle, however, such a complicated pattern can be resolved into a combination of regular wave patterns. The incidence of peaks at a point in the ocean in a transient encounter of different wave patterns results in unusually high peaks, and similarly the combination of the troughs gives a pronounced trough.

FIGURE 5–9 *The rough surface of the ocean is called "sea." Its texture is the result of the superposition of different regular wave patterns of variable direction, wave length and amplitude. (From the U.S. Naval Oceanographic Office Publication 603, "Practical Methods for Observing and Forecasting Ocean Waves by Means of Wave Spectra and Statistics," 1955.)*

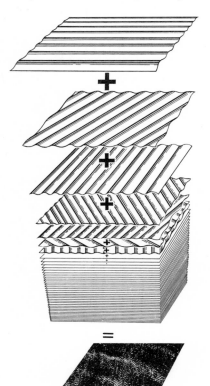

So far we have talked about waves that are not coupled to the bottom of the ocean. These are so-called deep-water waves. The moment waves or swells approach shallow water, they begin to feel bottom. The critical depth for this interaction to be significant is one-half the wave length of a wave or swell. When this criterion is met several effects are noticeable. The wave length decreases and the wave-peak height increases. This is the consequence of the simplified relationship, derived from classical hydrodynamic theory, that the velocity of a wave is proportional to the square root of the water depth. The exact relationship is dependent on the ratio of depth of water to wave length.

As the waves approach a coastline that has promontories and embayments, the wave front (or the imaginary line delineating the major linear trend of the modified waves) assumes a new pattern replicating the submerged features of the coast, as shown

The oceans in motion

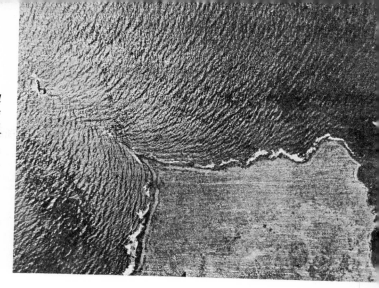

FIGURE 5-10 *As wind waves approach a coastline they will be refracted as the water become shallower. If the bottom gradient is the same in all directions from the complex shore line, the wave front will bend, to become parallel with the coastline. This photograph was taken at the north end of San Clemente Island, California, on June 20, 1944. (Official U.S. Naval photograph.)*

in Fig. 5-10. This bending of the waves is called refraction. It is due to the fact that the crest of a wave will move more slowly the shallower the water, hence the wave front will bend. It is evident that more of the energy of the wave will be concentrated on the headland than in the embayment, so there will be greater destruction and erosion of headlands than embayments. Indeed, if the sea were to win its battle of attrition, without any rejuvention of the land topography, the ultimate shoreline would be a straight one paralleling the contours of the submerged offshore shelf area.

As a wave approaches the shore, at some point the water molecules describing the circle of motion encounter resistance on the bottom of sufficient magnitude to cause the surface part of the circle to break, thus forming what are known as breakers. This occurs at the point where the depth equals about 1.3 times the wave height. After the breaking of the wave (in places the phenomenon occurs several times before the shore line is reached), the wave is expended on the shore as surf and swash.

Table 5-2

Sinusoidal Swells in Deep Water

Wave Length (in Feet)	Approximate Velocity (in Miles per Hour)
184	21
326	28
512	35
738	42
1,000	49
1,310	56

The oceans in motion

6

Marine geochemistry

We now turn to the oceans as a chemical system. In order to understand the chemical processes operating in the ocean we must try to evaluate the many different influences and interactions relating to it. The atmosphere, streams, sediments, and organisms, both marine and terrestrial—all have their role in determining the chemical properties of sea water. The study of their chemical interactions on a world-wide scale requires a knowledge of the distributions of the elements in the oceans, the types of chemical reactions that can occur in solutions, and a knowledge of the rates and mechanisms of supply and removal for each component.

The Distributions of the Elements in the Oceans

It is convenient to categorize the elements distributed in the oceans, in their various chemical states, into three groups: (1) the major elements, (2) the "nutrient" elements, and (3) the trace elements. The patterns of distribution of these three groups in the oceans are sufficiently different to make such a division useful. The major elements, as we have seen above, have approximately the same relative abundances throughout the oceans and a fairly narrow range of absolute concentration because the salinity of the open ocean varies only between narrow limits. This is not necessarily true, however, of the elements associated closely with living organisms such as carbon, oxygen, nitrogen, and phosphorus—the nutrient elements; nor is it true of the elements that occur in the parts-per-billion range of concentration—the trace elements.

Since we have discussed the major components of sea water in the previous chapter, attention now will be given to the nutrient and trace elements only.

The Nutrient Elements—
Carbon, Oxygen, Nitrogen, and Phosphorus

Aside from water, the most prominent compounds in plants and animals are those containing carbon, oxygen, nitrogen, and phosphorus, in the form of amino acids (which make up proteins), fats, starches, sugars, and the important phosphorus-containing compounds such as ATP (adenosine triphosphate) that are important for energy transfer within organisms. In the oceans, the constituent elements are available in solution as dissolved bicarbonate, phosphate, and nitrate.

The primary biological activity in the oceans, as on land, is the fixing of carbon by photosynthesis. All other life in the oceans depends on this first step. As we have seen, this process is accomplished primarily by single-celled organisms whose shells are commonly preserved in deep-sea sediments.

Carbon, nitrogen, and phosphorus are extracted from solution in the top hundred meters of the ocean where enough light penetrates for photosynthesis. The food chain then continues through a sequence of organisms living mainly in the surface layers, but some organic particles settle through the water. In the deeper waters bacterial action destroys much of this fine organic material and returns the nutrient elements to ionic form. The result of these events is that the surface waters are depleted in the dissolved nutrient elements and the deeper waters are enriched. If the nutrient elements were not returned to the surface waters, the concentration would soon become so low that the primary productivity would be diminished. At rates of biological productivity determined for the oceans, this depletion would lead to a virtually lifeless sea in less than a year.

As we have seen in the previous chapter, however, the region of the thermocline indicates mixing of the deeper water with the surface water through eddy diffusion and convection. This mixing occurs rapidly enough to supply the nutrient elements at the same rate at which they are lost by biological action. The resulting steady-state concentration gradients of phosphate and the other nutrient elements (Fig. 6–1) reflect the process of removal of dissolved nurients from the surface waters, transport downward as particles, regeneration, and resupply by mixing. In areas of upwelling, water from depths down to 300 meters is even more rapidly brought to the surface, thus supplying nutrient elements at a faster rate than that of normal eddy diffusion and small-scale convection. This upwelling results in a greatly enhanced biological productivity.

The cycle of the nutrient elements is shown diagrammatically in Fig. 6–2. In biological processes oxygen plays an important role either as the by-product of photosynthesis or as a requirement for metabolism. The oxygen concentrations observed in sea water are close to those expected if equilibrium for gas distributions were established between surface ocean water and the atmosphere. For example, the cold Antarctic Bottom Water was formed in the Antarctic in contact with the atmosphere hence should have a relatively high oxygen concentration. Yet values larger than the saturation value of oxygen are encountered in surface layers because of the production of oxygen by photosynthesis. Deeper, however, where photosynthesis is no longer possible, organic compounds are burned for food with the help of dissolved oxygen, thus causing a decrease in the dissolved oxygen concentration to values below saturation.

If aeration by advection, convection, or eddy diffusion is too slow, compared

FIGURE 6–1 *Vertical distribution of the nutrient components, phosphate and nitrate, in the Atlantic, Pacific, and Indian Oceans. (After Sverdrup, Johnson, and Fleming, 1942.)*

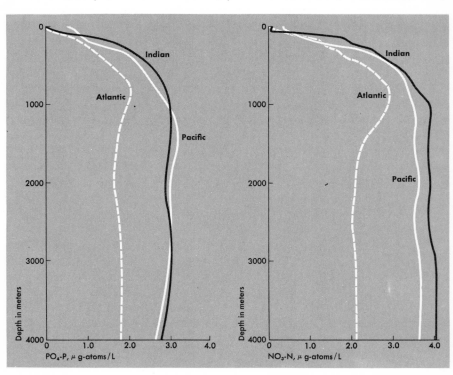

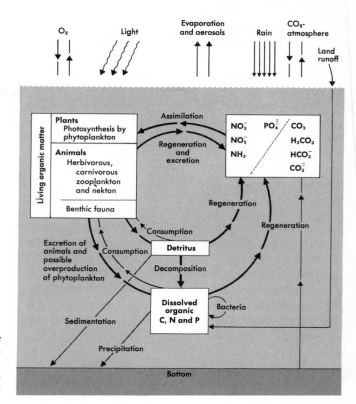

FIGURE 6-2 A schematic diagram of the biogeochemical cycles of phosphorus, nitrogen, carbon, and oxygen. (After Duursma, 1961.)

to the rate at which biologically useable organic material is supplied, the oxygen is rapidly used up and stagnation results at depth. Deep oceanic basins such as the Black Sea, the Cariaco deep in the Caribbean, and fjords are examples of such areas. Under stagnant conditions the organic compounds are utilized by certain bacteria that obtain oxygen by reducing the plentiful sulfate ion ($SO_4^=$) in sea water to hydrogen sulfide (H_2S). This process also occurs off the seashore in muds where aeration is inhibited.

Trace Elements

Most of the trace elements found in sea water occur in very low concentrations, as can be seen in Table 6-1. The concentration levels are probably controlled by the direct or indirect action of organisms. Planktonic organisms tend to concentrate many of the trace elements out of sea water, as was shown in Table 3-3, and certain trace elements, such as copper, zinc, cobalt, iron and molybdenum, are known to be important in biological systems. Copper is required, for instance, in the blood of several groups of invertebrates (for example, the molluscs and the crustacea), and cobalt is an important ingredient of vitamin B_{12}. There are some unusual concentrations of elements in specific organisms as well. One species of radiolarian, for example, deposits a shell composed of strontium sulfate, and barium sulfate has been found in the tissue

Table 6-1

The Composition of Sea Water at 35 ‰ Salinity

Element	Symbol	1961 Atomic Weight	Micrograms per Liter	Element	Symbol	1961 Atomic Weight	Micrograms per Liter
Hydrogen	H	1.00797	1.10×10^8	Molybdenum	Mo	95.94	10
Helium	He	4.0026	0.0072	Ruthenium	Ru	101.07	
Lithium	Li	6.939	170	Rhodium	Rh	102.905	
Beryllium	Be	9.0133	0.0006	Palladium	Pd	106.4	
Boron	B	10.811	4,450	Silver	Ag	107.870	0.28
Carbon (inorganic)	C	12.01115	28,000	Cadmium	Cd	112.40	0.11
(dissolved organic)			2,000	Indium	In	114.82	
Nitrogen (dissolved N_2)		14.0067	15,500	Tin	Sn	118.69	0.81
(as NO_3^-, NO_2^-, NH_4^+)			670	Antimony	Sb	121.75	0.33
Oxygen (dissolved O_2)		15.9994	6,000	Tellurium	Te	127.60	
(as H_2O)			8.83×10^8	Iodine	I	126.9044	64
Fluorine	F	18.9984	1300	Xenon	Xe	131.30	0.047
Neon	Ne	20.183	0.120	Cesium	Cs	132.905	0.30
Sodium	Na	22.9898	1.08×10^7	Barium	Ba	137.34	21
Magnesium	Mg	24.312	1.29×10^6	Lanthanum	La	138.91	0.0029
Aluminum	Al	26.9815	1	Cerium	Ce	140.12	0.0013
Silicon	Si	28.086	2900	Praseodymium	Pr	140.907	0.00064
Phosphorus	P	30.9738	88	Neodymium	Nd	144.24	0.0023
Sulfur	S	32.064	9.04×10^5	Samarium	Sm	150.35	0.00042
Chlorine	Cl	35.453	1.94×10^7	Europium	Eu	151.96	0.000114
Argon	Ar	39.948	450	Gadolinium	Gd	157.25	0.0006
Potassium	K	39.102	3.92×10^5	Terbium	Tb	158.924	0.0009
Calcium	Ca	40.08	4.11×10^5	Dysprosium	Dy	162.50	0.00073
Scandium	Sc	44.956	<0.004	Holmium	Ho	164.930	0.00022
Titanium	Ti	47.90	1	Erbium	Er	167.26	0.00061
Vanadium	V	50.942	1.9	Thulium	Tm	168.934	0.00013
Chromium	Cr	51.996	0.2	Ytterbium	Yb	173.04	0.00052
Manganese	Mn	54.9381	1.9	Lutetium	Lu	174.97	0.00012
Iron	Fe	55.847	3.4	Hafnium	Hf	178.49	<0.008
Cobalt	Co	58.9332	0.39	Tantalum	Ta	180.948	<0.0025
Nickel	Ni	58.71	6.6	Tungsten	W	183.85	<0.001
Copper	Cu	63.54	23	Rhenium	Re	186.2	
Zinc	Zn	65.37	11	Osmium	Os	190.2	
Gallium	Ga	69.72	0.03	Iridium	Ir	192.2	
Germanium	Ge	72.59	0.06	Platinum	Pt	195.09	
Arsenic	As	74.9216	2.6	Gold	Au	196.967	0.011
Selenium	Se	78.96	0.090	Mercury	Hg	200.59	0.15
Bromine	Br	79.909	6.73×10^4	Thallium	Tl	204.37	
Krypton	Kr	83.80	0.21	Lead	Pb	207.19	0.03
Rubidium	Rb	85.47	120	Bismuth	Bi	208.980	0.02
Strontium	Sr	87.62	8,100	Radium	Ra	(226)	1×10^{-13}
Yttrium	Y	88.905	0.003	Thorium	Th	232.038	0.0015
Zirconium	Zr	91.22	0.026	Protactinium	Pa	(231)	2×10^{-10}
Niobium	Nb	92.906	0.015	Uranium	U	238.03	3.3

of another group of unicellular organisms. Nickel is peculiarly concentrated by sponges.

On the basis of these facts, we would expect to see variations in the marine concentrations of some trace elements that resemble those of the nutrient elements. In some parts of the ocean where upwelling is prominent the concentrations of some trace elements increase with depth, but otherwise there

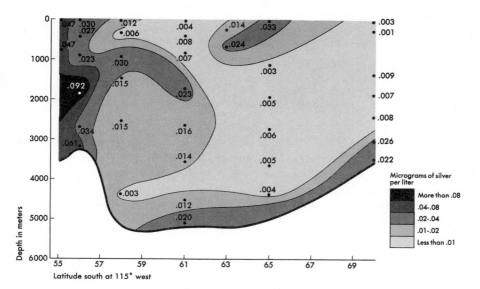

FIGURE 6–3 *The distribution of silver in Antarctic waters at 115° W. The concentration increases towards the north. A profile at about 90° W shows a similar distribution. (After Schutz and Turekian, 1965.)*

is no ocean-wide correlation with biological productivity or phosphate concentration. For example, Fig. 6–3 is one of two similar profiles of silver concentration in the east Pacific sector of the Antarctic and shows an increase in silver concentration from the ice front northward to the main part of the Pacific. Biological activity is high in the Antarctic because of the high phosphorus concentration, but the concentration of silver is lowest of all the oceans, and sediments do not indicate a high rate of silver extraction by organisms. In fact, there are strong regional variations in the concentration of silver, cobalt, and nickel, as seen in Table 6–2. Yet other trace elements like rubidium, cesium, and molybdenum are fairly constant in concentration from one location in the ocean to another. Hence, we cannot make any generalizations regarding trace elements, and must depend on the observed empirical variations for now.

Table 6–2

Regional Averages of Silver, Cobalt, and Nickel in the Oceans*

Region	Silver	Cobalt	Nickel
Caribbean Sea	0.25	0.078	2.1
Gulf of Mexico	0.16	0.84	2.0
Labrador Sea	0.13	0.16	4.9
Northwest Atlantic	0.19	0.21	3.5
Northeast Atlantic	0.25	0.13	3.1
Southwest Atlantic	0.18	0.22	4.8
Southeast Atlantic	0.64	0.25	19.2
Indian Ocean	0.69	1.4	5.4
Central Pacific	0.34	0.75	20
East Pacific	0.23	0.18	5.5
Antarctic (East Pacific sector)	0.017	0.031	1.6

Schutz and Turekian, 1965.

* Concentrations are expressed as micrograms per liter.

Marine geochemistry

93

Factors Controlling the Chemical State of the Ocean

In a description of the chemical state of the oceans three properties are of fundamental importance: (1) the concentrations of the principal ions, (2) the acidity, and (3) the oxidation-reduction potential. If we know what controls these properties, we can then see how they influence the concentration of the majority of the elements in sea water and the composition of sediments.

Solubility and Ions

If we dissolve 35 grams of household salt (sodium chloride) in one liter of tap water, the resulting solution resembles sea water in concentration except for the other dissolved substances. But what does it mean when we say that sodium chloride dissolves? We know that the sodium chloride solution conducts an electrical current very efficiently, whereas pure distilled water does not. Hence, the salt solution must contain charged particles capable of carrying the current, since all electricity involves the movement of electrically charged particles. From this we infer that the sodium chloride has dissociated into charged particles in the solution. We can write the reaction:

$$NaCl \text{ (solid)} + water = Na^+ \text{ (aqueous)} + Cl^- \text{ (aqueous)}$$

The electric conductors in solution are called *ions*; the positively charged ion (Na^+) is called a *cation* since it is attracted to a negatively charged cathode, and the negatively charged ion (Cl^-) is called an *anion* since it is attracted to a positively charged anode.

If we keep stirring more and more salt into our solution, eventually, after a certain point, if the temperature has been kept constant, all subsequently added salt accumulates at the bottom of the container. At this point we say that the solution is *saturated* with respect to sodium chloride. Saturation means that a definite amount of salt will go into solution for a given volume of solvent and a given temperature. This implies an equilibrium state, in chemical terms, and a constant can be defined then to describe this condition. It is called an *equilibrium constant*. In the case of the solution of a salt the equilibrium constant is called the *solubility product constant*. For a saturated sodium chloride solution, for instance, the K_{SP} is equal to the product of the concentrations of the sodium and chloride ions. (The brackets indicate concentrations.)

$$K_{SP} = [Na^+] \times [Cl^-] \text{ (the notation "aqueous" is dropped because it is self evident)}$$

The general rule regarding solubility can now be restated for compounds like sodium chloride as follows: A solution is *saturated* with regard to a particular solid phase if the product of the concentrations of the ions that make up the solid phase is equal to the solubility product constant. The important point here is that the *product* of the ionic concentrations is the critical thing, not the individual ionic concentrations. Concentrations are commonly given in *moles per liter,* a mole being the mass, in grams, equal to the atomic weight of the element. A mole of any two elements has the same number of atoms.

For instance if a salt MX (the term "salt" is used for all solid compounds of ions and is not restricted to common sodium chloride) has a solubility product constant (K_{SP}) of 0.01, then the products of $[M^+] \times [X^-]$ shown in Table 6–3 will all be saturated solutions with respect to the compound MX.

With a logical extension of the solubility product constant calculation, we can apply it to salts of diversely charged cations and anions.

Normal sea water is undersaturated with regard to all of the major salts that can be formed from the combination of the major ions, except for calcium carbonate in surface waters. That is, the solubility product constants of such salts as $CaSO_4$, $MgSO_4$, KCl, $NaCl$, to name some of the more important possibilities, are not exceeded in normal sea water. If we increase the concentrations of the ions by evaporation, various salts will precipitate as the solubility product constant of each is exceeded.

It is evident that the concentrations of the major components of sea water, in particular the anions, set the maximum concentration levels of the minor and trace elements on the basis of solubility product constants of the most insoluble compounds.

Many of the elements found in trace quantities in sea water can form complexes with the dominant anions, thereby increasing their solubility above what is predicted by the solubility product constant of the most insoluble salt. Hence, although silver chloride is extremely insoluble in distilled water, its solubility increases in a sodium chloride solution by several orders of magnitude. Even though the concentration of Ag^+ is diminished by the increased chloride-ion concentration, the concentrations of complex chloride complexes such as $AgCl_2^-$ are high enough to increase the total amount of dissolved silver.

Salts generally have larger empirical solubility product constants in saline water than in distilled (or stream) water even if special complexes are not formed. For instance, the empirical solubility product constant of barium sulfate is 10^{-10} in distilled water (or streams) but about 10^{-8} in sea water. As it happens, the sulfate-ion concentration of sea water is about 100 times that of streams hence the barium concentrations for sea water and streams should be about the same to give empirical solubility product constants of

Table 6–3

Saturated Solutions
of Salt MX $(K_{SP} = 0.01)$

[M+]	[X−]	$K_{SP} = [M^+][X^-]$
10	0.001	0.01
1	0.01	0.01
0.1	0.1	0.01
0.01	1	0.01
0.001	10	0.01

Marine geochemistry

Table 6–4

Solubility Controls on Concentration of Trace Elements in Sea Water

Element	Insoluble Salt in Normal Sea Water	Expected Concentration (Log Moles/L)*	Oberved Concentration (Log Moles/L)	Expected Concentration in Sulfide-Rich Sea Water or Mud (Log Moles/L)*
Lanthanum	$LaPO_4$	-11.1	-10.7	——
Thorium	$Th_3(PO_4)_4$	-11.8	-11.7	——
Cobalt	$CoCO_3$	-6.5	-8.2	-12.1
Nickel	$Ni(OH)_2$	-3.2	-6.9	-10.7
Copper	$Cu(OH)_2$	-5.8	-7.3	-26.0
Silver°°	$AgCl$	-4.2	-8.5	-19.8
Zinc	$ZnCO_3$	-3.7	-6.8	-14.1
Cadmium	$CdCO_3$	-5.0	-9.0	-16.2
Mercury°°	$Hg(OH)_2$	$+1.9$	-9.1	-43.7
Lead°°	$PbCO_3$	-5.6	-9.8	-16.6

° The expected concentrations at 25°C. are calculated on the basis of the following thermodynamic concentrations, a ("activities") of the anions: $\log a_{PO_4^=} = -9.3$, $\log a_{CO_3^=} = -5.3$, $\log a_{OH^-} = -6$, $\log a_{S^=} = -9$.

°° Form strong chloride complexes.

10^{-8} and 10^{-10} respectively. Table 6–4 gives a list of the most insoluble compounds of some trace elements in sea water together with the maximum concentrations of the trace elements compatible with the major anionic composition of sea water. For comparison, the observed concentrations of these elements are also given. It is evident that, on this basis, the oceans are generally undersaturated with regard to the trace elements as well as the major elements except possibly lanthanum (and the other rare-earth metals) and thorium. In reducing environments, however, the solubility product constants of most of the metal sulfides are exceeded.

The Acidity of the Ocean

The acidity of a solution is determined by the concentration of hydrogen ions (H^+). The water molecule, composed of hydrogen and oxygen, can form ions by dissociation much as the inorganic compounds or salts do when put into solution. For salts like sodium chloride the dissociation is complete for all practical purposes. The degree of dissociation of water, however, is far from complete. The dissociation of water is written:

$$H_2O \text{ (liquid)} = H^+ \text{ (aqueous)} + OH^- \text{ (aqueous)}$$

Marine geochemistry

The equilibrium product constant for this reaction is written in a manner similar to that for the solubility product constant:

$$K_{\text{dissociation}} = [\text{H}^+]\,[\text{OH}^-]$$

In pure water, for every hydrogen (H^+) ion formed by dissociation, a hydroxyl (OH^-) ion must be formed; the concentration of each is the same. The value of $K_{\text{dissociation}}$ at atmospheric pressure and 25°C is about 10^{-14}, hence the *hydrogen-ion concentration* of pure water is 10^{-7}.

Commonly, purely as a matter of convenience, the hydrogen-ion-concentration scale is converted to logarithmic form (base 10) so as to avoid writing exponents. Such a scale is called the *pH scale:* pH is defined as the negative logarithm of the hydrogen-ion concentration. A pH of 7 corresponds to a hydrogen-ion concentration of 10^{-7} and is the pH of pure water. A lesser pH value is considered acidic, a greater one is basic. Since the pH of seawater is around 8, the ocean can be considered as a slightly basic solution.

In the laboratory, the pH of water can be lowered by adding an acid, such as hydrochloric acid or acetic acid (vinegar), since on dissociation it adds hydrogen ions without adding hydroxyl ions; pH can be raised by adding a base, such as sodium hydroxide (lye) or ammonium hydroxide (ammonia water).

The chemical species involved in the regulation of the pH of ocean water are also common compounds: carbon dioxide in the air, carbonic acid, and calcium carbonate. Carbon dioxide gas is the respiratory waste of animals and the starting point for photosynthesis in land plants. When carbon dioxide is bubbled through water, it dissolves to form carbonic acid, thus lowering the pH of the solution. This carbonic acid will react vigorously with calcium carbonate, with an increase in the pH. The reaction is: $\text{H}_2\text{CO}_3 + \text{CaCO}_3 = \text{Ca}^{++} + 2\text{HCO}_3^-$. It is evident that hydrogen ions from the dissociation of the carbonic acid are in part used up to form bicarbonate ions (HCO_3^-) from carbonate ions ($\text{CO}_3^=$) that are derived from the dissociation of the CaCO_3. This action tends to regulate the pH of the solution, hence we say the solution is "buffered." More precisely, the series of chemical reactions described above and their intermediate steps can be expressed in the following equations, shown with their associated equilibrium constants (including the dissociation constants and solubility product constants) at 25°C.

$K_P = 10^{-1.47}$	CO_2 (gas) $+ \text{H}_2\text{O}$ (liquid) $= \text{H}_2\text{CO}_3$ (aqueous)
$K_1 = 10^{-6.4}$	H_2CO_3 (aqueous) $= \text{H}^+$ (aqueous) $+ \text{HCO}_3^-$ (aqueous)
$K_2 = 10^{-10.3}$	HCO_3^- (aqueous) $= \text{H}^+$ (aqueous) $+ \text{CO}_3^=$ (aqueous)
$K_{SP} = 10^{-8.3}$	CaCO_3 (solid) $+ \text{H}_2\text{O}$ (liquid) $= \text{Ca}^{++}$ (aqueous) $+ \text{CO}_3^=$ (aqueous)
$K_W = 10^{-14}$	H_2O (liquid) $= \text{H}^+$ (aqueous) $+ \text{OH}^-$ (aqueous)

On the basis of these equations and the dissociation of water we can relate the pressure of carbon dioxide in the atmosphere to the acidity of sea water on

Marine geochemistry

the basis of equilibrium with calcium carbonate, which is given by the following simplified equation:

$$P_{CO_2} = (K_P K_1)^{-1} \left(\frac{2K_{SP}}{K_2} \right)^{\frac{1}{2}} [H^+]^{\frac{3}{2}}$$

The present-day pressure of carbon dioxide is 0.0003 atmospheres, corresponding to a pH of about 8 for seawater, the value which is, in fact, found. Rather large changes in the carbon dioxide pressure result in only small changes in the pH.

An interesting question arises from the relationship between the pressure of carbon dioxide in the air and the pH of seawater: Is the carbon dioxide pressure determining the pH or is the pH determining the carbon dioxide pressure?

The argument that the carbon dioxide pressure is independently determined and thus influences the pH of sea water is based on the premise that it is the maintenance, by respiration, of the supply of carbon dioxide in the atmosphere which is the critical factor. Hence, it is argued, as the result of the balance of life processes producing and using carbon dioxide, a steady-state level of carbon dioxide is maintained in the atmosphere.

The alternative view is that reactions of silicates in the oceanic sediments control the hydrogen-ion concentration. This control can be effected either by direct reaction of hydrogen ions with the clay minerals so as to transform them from one kind to another or by simple exchange with the cations at adsorption sites in the clay minerals. In order to understand the basis of these reactions in controling the acidity of sea water, we must understand the mode of origin of the clay minerals in sediments. These are ultimately the products of weathering as was indicated in Chapter 3. We can write a generalized weathering reaction (resulting primarily from the action of life) in the following way:

$$Na^+ \text{ feldspar} + H^+ \text{(aqueous)} = \text{kaolinite} + Na^+ \text{(aqueous)} + SiO_2 \text{(aqueous)}$$

and an equilibrium constant can be written for this reaction:

$$K = \frac{[Na^+][SiO_2]}{[H^+]}$$

In the oceanic realm it is presumed that the same reaction is also occurring, but mainly in the reverse direction—that is, kaolinite would react with the large amount of sodium in the sea to produce an idealized sodium feldspar. No matter which direction we approach the reaction from, it is evident that the proportions of the different ions in solution will be controled by the equilibrium constant. This constant would control the hydrogen-ion concentration and hence the carbon dioxide pressure in the atmosphere.

Unfortunately, we have no evidence that such reactions actually do occur in sea water, so we do not know if their role in determining the pH of sea water is important.

Marine geochemistry

Oxidation-Reduction in the Ocean

A piece of steel exposed to the atmosphere and rain undergoes oxidation, resulting in a product we call rust, which is composed of the minerals goethite (FeOOH) and possibly hematite (Fe_2O_3). A simplified equation for this is:

$$2\,Fe^0\ (\text{metallic iron}) + \tfrac{3}{2}O_2 = Fe_2O_3\ (\text{hematite})$$

This reaction can also be written as the sum of two half-reactions: one in which the iron is oxidized and the other in which the oxygen is reduced. Oxidation is the loss of electrons, reduction is the gain of electrons. Hence, an "oxidation-reduction reaction" actually involves a transfer of electrons.

Oxidation: $2\,Fe^0\ (\text{metallic iron}) = 2\,Fe^{+3} + 6\ \text{electrons}$

Reduction: $\tfrac{3}{2}O_2{}^0 + 6\ \text{electrons} = 3\,O^{-2}$

Sum of half reactions: $2\,Fe^0 + \tfrac{3}{2}O_2 = Fe_2O_3$

In our atmosphere the oxygen pressure is so large, and maintained thus as the result of photosynthesis, that the oxidation of metallic iron proceeds to completion. If we had a closed system, however, and a limited amount of available oxygen, the reaction would convert to iron oxide enough metallic iron to lower the oxygen pressure to an equilibrium value.

Since electrons are transferred in oxidation-reduction reactions, if we could imagine that the reaction takes place by the transfer of the electrons through a wire with a voltmeter connected across the wire, we would see a voltage potential difference between the two half-cells until the reaction had reached equilibrium. Hence, we can think of each half-cell as having a voltage potential. At equilibrium the oxidation potential would just equal the reduction potential. Of course, what we have been talking about has been put into practical use in the form of batteries. Equilibrium in a battery means a dead battery. The oxidation-reduction potential of a half-reaction relative to the oxidation-reduction potential of the idealized half-reaction (shown below) is called the Eh.

$$\tfrac{1}{2}H_2 \xrightarrow{\ 1\ \text{atm.}\ } H^+\ (\text{aqueous; thermodynamically equal to 1 mole per liter}) + \text{electron}$$

In our convention a positive Eh indicates that the half-reaction will couple with another half-cell and be reduced at the expense of the oxidation of the other species.

In normal sea water the half-reaction that determines the oxidation-reduction potential (Eh) of sea water is:

$$2\,H_2O = 4\ \text{electrons} + O_2 + 4\,H^+$$

Marine geochemistry

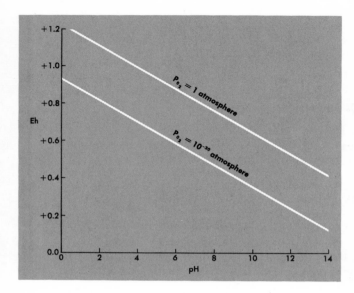

FIGURE 6–4 *The relationship of pH, Eh and the partial pressure of oxygen in the atmosphere. Although P_{O_2} is actually equal to 0.2 atmospheres instead of one atmosphere, the difference between the two lines is almost imperceptible. The relationship for P_{O_2} equal to 10^{-20} atmospheres is drawn for reference. The lines represent the half-cell: $2H_2O = 4$ electrons $+ O_2 + 4H^+$. At a pH $= 8$ and 0.2 atmosphere P_{O_2} the Eh is about 0.75 volts.*

All reactions in open sea water involving the transfer of electrons are controled by this half-cell, and the Eh is fixed because the pressure of oxygen and the hydrogen-ion concentration are determined for the ocean (Fig. 6–4).

Generally, ocean water is a highly oxidizing solution so that for many elements the higher oxidation states exist in solution. In nearshore areas and restricted basins, however, the effect of organisms in depleting the dissolved oxygen content is to lower the Eh and result in more reduced states of some of the elements. Chromium, for example, exists primarily as $CrO_4^=$ (Cr^{+6}) in aerated sea water but becomes Cr^{+3} in reducing environments.

Material Balance

Let us now follow what happens to several of the major components of sea water as they are derived from the continents by weathering and stream transport. Our summary will resemble a balance sheet or a budget, in which we determine the source and quantity of each component and its disposition in the ocean.

The Composition and Supply Rate of Streams

The total annual supply of dissolved material from the streams of the world is 36×10^{14} grams. The composition of streams varies around the Earth because of differences in climate and types of local rock; nevertheless the average concentration of the major ions in streams given in Table 6–5 is a reasonable starting point for our discussion.

Sodium, potassium, and silica (SiO_2) are derived from common silicate minerals such as the feldspars (K, Na aluminosilicate) by the action of carbonic acid, which is itself derived from the action of bacteria on organic material. A typical reaction, written above on page 98 without considering the role of carbon, is rewritten:

$$\text{Na feldspar} + H_2O + CO_2 = \text{kaolinite} + Na^+ + HCO_3^- + SiO_2$$

In some streams it has been found that the concentrations of silica and of sodium and bicarbonate ions, along with the presence of kaolinite in the sediments, are compatible with the expected equilibrium concentrations based on the above reaction.

Calcium and magnesium are derived primarily from the weathering of limestones and dolomites although a small amount is supplied by the disintegration of silicate minerals. The main agent of decomposition again is carbonic acid derived from life processes in the soil. The reaction for calcium is written:

$$CaCO_3 + H_2O + CO_2 = Ca^{++} + 2\,HCO_3^-$$

The last major ion is sulfate ($SO_4^=$), which is in part also responsible for the solution of limestones and dolomites by the formation of soluble calcium and magnesium sulfate. The sulfate is formed by the oxidation of iron sulfide (pyrite), which is found as an important accessory mineral in many rock types, including sedimentary deposits. The reactions for calcium would be:

$$4\,FeS + 9\,O_2 + 4\,H_2O = 2\,Fe_2O_3 + 4\,H_2SO_4$$
$$\text{and} \quad H_2SO_4 + CaCO_3 = Ca^{++} + SO_4^= + H_2O + CO_2$$

In addition to these ions derived directly from the weathering of rocks a certain amount of wind-transported sea salt is rained out on drainage basins, thus providing some of the chloride ions found in streams. Most of the chloride appears to come from the leaching of salts associated with sedimentary rocks.

The dissolved load of streams, as well as the sediments, brought to the oceans must ultimately be removed from the water if a steady-state composition is to be maintained. We have already seen that many of the trace elements occur in sea water at levels far below the concentrations expected from the solubility of the most insoluble salt of the element. This implies efficient removal of the elements by

Table 6–5

Average Composition of Streams

Component	Milligrams per Liter
HCO_3^-	58.4
$SO_4^=$	11.2
Cl^-	7.8
NO_3^-	1.0
Ca^{++}	15.
Mg^{++}	4.1
Na^+	6.3
K^+	2.3
(Fe)	(0.67)
SiO_2	13.1
Total	120

Livingstone, 1963.

Marine geochemistry

other methods to keep the level low. Table 6–4 shows that the concentration levels observed in sea water are more in accord with the values expected in equilibrium with strongly reducing areas where sulfide ions are generated, namely the sediments of nearshore areas and stagnant basins.

But by far the most massive removal processes involve the elements calcium, magnesium, sodium, potassium, carbon, sulfur, and silica. Our next sections deal with the mode of removal of these elements in the marine realm.

The Marine Budget of Calcium

Calcium is removed from ocean water mainly by the deposition of calcium carbonate by marine organisms. Where does this take place? In nearshore deposits of molluscan shells and coral reefs (with their associated deposits) or in the deep-sea environment as coccoliths and foraminiferan shells? It is not possible to make an accurate survey of nearshore deposition rates because of the great variability of nearshore calcium carbonate fixation and sediment accumulation. It is possible, however, to determine the average accumulation rate of calcium carbonate in the deep oceans.

In Chapter 4 we saw that rates of accumulation of clay and calcium carbonate components were determined in a large number of cores raised from the Atlantic Ocean based on radiocarbon dating and paleontologic correlation. Since most of these cores were, by design, rich in calcium carbonate, they represent a biased sampling of calcium carbonate rates. The correct method of determining the calcium carbonate accumulation rate in the Atlantic Ocean is to use the average clay accumulation rate and the average calcium carbonate concentration of the deep-sea sediments, from data of the sort presented graphically in Figs. 3–3 and 3–4. The results of this type of estimation are presented in Table 6–6. It is doubtful that the total deep-sea accumulation rate of calcium carbonate in all the oceans other than the Atlantic is less than half that of the Atlantic or more than equal to it. In any case, the total rate is in the

Table 6–6

Calcium Carbonate Balance in the Oceans

Ocean	Average Percentage of $CaCO_3$ in Deep-sea Sediments	Average Clay Accumulation Rate (g/cm^2 1,000 Years)	Total $CaCO_3$ Accumulation Rate ($10^{16}g$ $CaCO_3$/1,000 Years)
Atlantic Ocean	43.7	1.20	77
Pacific Ocean	37.8	0.30?	30
Indian Ocean and all others seas			30
Total			137

Rates of Atlantic Ocean and all other oceans equal	154
Rate of all other oceans equal to half the Atlantic Ocean rate	115
Stream supply	122

range of values calculated for calcium carbonate supply from the continents by streams. This calculation implies that the amount of calcium carbonate removed on the continental shelves is indeterminably small.

Let us consider the long-term balance of calcium carbonate. At present rates of accumulation in the deep sea, it will take about 100 million years for all the calcium carbonate that has been deposited as limestones throughout geologic time and is now exposed above sea level on the continents to be removed and deposited in the deep sea, where presumably it is no longer available for recycling through uplift. Such calculations, far from speaking for catastrophic changes in terrestrial conditions, compel a search for mechanisms of redistribution of calcium carbonate over geologic time by other means than uplift and erosion. If we assume that the sea is saturated with regard to calcium carbonate at the surface but undersaturated at depth, then a transfer of calcium carbonate from the bottom by re-solution may be effected as long as the oceans circulate. Some of this will always be deposited on continental margins or in interior seas, the quantity being determined by the amounts of such areas at any particular time.

If, just prior to the Cambrian Period 600 million years ago, before interior seas and continental shelf areas became extensive, the continents had been "washed clean" of calcium carbonate, and if the amount of calcium carbonate dissolved in the oceans was about the same then as now, the main area of deposition for several hundred million years before the beginning of the Cambrian Period must have been the deep sea. At the onset of the Cambrian Period, however, with the extensive development of shallow-water areas and the evolution therein of a large number of organisms that deposited calcium carbonate, the transfer of calcium carbonate from the deep-sea bottom to the shallow-water areas progressed.

The Marine Budget of Carbon

For each calcium or magnesium ion dissolved from limestone, two bicarbonate ions are formed. Since only one of these is required in the precipitation of calcium carbonate, the other must be accounted for in another fashion to avoid increasing the concentration in the oceans. The path is biological for the most part, for marine plants utilize the bicarbonate ion directly from sea water in photosynthesis. After this initial fixation of carbon and a series of other steps, carbon dioxide is released to the atmosphere through the respiration of marine organisms. Thus, for each molecule of calcium carbonate precipitated, one molecule of carbon dioxide is ultimately released to the atmosphere.

The Marine Budgets of Sodium and Potassium

As we have seen, the bicarbonate ion is also a product of the weathering of silicates. If no reactions took place in the ocean with the sodium and potassium that are derived from the weathering of silicates, the sea would accumulate sodium and potassium bicarbonate and its pH would climb up and up until the highly basic solution would destroy a large part of the marine life. Obviously this is not happening now, nor, to judge from the paleontologic evidence at our disposal, did it happen in the past. What then is the mechanism whereby sodium and potassium ions are removed and hydrogen ions released to combine with the bicarbonate, thus allowing the escape of carbon dioxide? One class of reactions involves the reconstitution of clay minerals. For instance:

$$\text{kaolinite} + SiO_2 + Na^+ + HCO_3^- = \text{Na feldspar} + CO_2 + H_2O$$

Alternatively, a mineral acid such as hydrochloric acid might be added from volcanoes at the same rate as sodium bicarbonate is added and thus neutralize the solution according to the symbolic reaction:

$$Na^+ + HCO_3^- + HCl = Na^+ + Cl^- + H_2O + CO_2$$

Simultaneously the silica is being removed biologically, as discussed below.

Sodium and potassium might also be exchanged on clay minerals by the release of calcium ions which then are precipitated as calcium carbonate with the release of a molecule of carbon dioxide.

The Marine Budget of Magnesium

It has been observed that river clays when put in contact with sea water will release calcium and hydrogen ions and absorb magnesium ions preferentially. The amount of exchange is not sufficient to account for all the magnesium brought to the sea with its associated bicarbonate (or sulfate— which is essentially replaced by the bicarbonate ion in sea water by the action of sulfate-reducing organisms). This then requires that magnesium bicarbonate be removed, either by the precipitation of magnesium carbonate as dolomite or high magnesium calcite or by the incorporation of magnesium hydroxide in the transformation of montmorillonite to chlorite. Neither of these processes, however, has yet been demonstrated as quantitatively important in the present-day seas. Since we have shown that most of the calcium carbonate is deposited in the deep sea, the fact that these carbonates are extremely low in magnesium ion ($<0.05\%$ Mg) discounts magnesium removal by deep-sea carbonate deposition. It is tempting to continue the search among silicate reactions.

The Marine Budget of Silica

There are two major ways in which silica is removed from sea water: (1) by inorganic reactions with the clay minerals, and (2) by organic removal by diatoms, radiolaria, and other organisms.

Although the evidence is circumstantial, it appears that silica is removed at least in part by reaction with clay minerals. The best argument proposed for this type of removal is that when clay minerals are put into a sea water solution containing silica in concentration greater than that in the sea, the silica concentration is decreased. This appears to be happening, in nature, along the Mississippi delta, where silica-rich, muddy Mississippi River water mixes with Gulf of Mexico water. This effect is not evident at the mouths of other large rivers, in part probably because the amount of clay minerals is low compared to the Mississippi.

The evidence for biological removal is direct, as we have seen in Chapter 3. Aside from the Antarctic, Arctic, and Pacific Equatorial sites of intense biological accumulation of silica, there are nearshore areas where silica is also efficiently removed from sea water. In fjords and embayments like Long Island Sound, silica is actually extracted from the open ocean as well as from the fresh-water sources—all due to the action of diatoms primarily. The most spectacular example of deposition in such environments is the Gulf of California, where the total rate of silica deposition exceeds the supply from streams by a factor of 100, indicating that it is being pumped in from the open ocean.

There is another source of silica aside from streams—glaciated areas such as Antarctica. Silicate minerals, including quartz, pulverized by the grinding action of moving glaciers are highly susceptible to solution.

The Marine Budget of Sulfur

Sulfur is brought to the oceans as the sulfate ion. Although it is utilized by deep-sea organisms in essential organic compounds, the concentration in sea water is sufficiently high to be unaffected by the normal oceanic biological cycles. In stagnant areas of the deep ocean, such as the deeper waters of the Black Sea discussed earlier, sulfate-reducing bacteria lower the sulfate concentration of sea water by producing hydrogen sulfide.

Sulfate reduction occurs to a larger degree in stagnant muds in shallow waters on the continental shelf where the organic content is especially high. The hydrogen sulfide produced in the sediments does not commonly reach the overlying ocean water in great abundance because it reacts readily with iron oxide in the sediments to produce black iron sulfide. When tides are especially low or waves churn the sediments, hydrogen sulfide may escape and make its presence known by its characteristic rotten-egg smell.

Sulfate may also be removed from sea water by precipitation as calcium sulfate in areas of evaporation such as the Persian Gulf or the "salinas" of Mexico. Deposits of gypsum ($CaSO_4 \cdot 2H_2O$) are formed at low temperatures in these environments and evaporite formations are preserved.

7

The history
of oceans and ocean basins

We now come to questions that are as simple as those of a child and, as is often the case with children's questions, as difficult to answer: (1) Where did all the water come from? (2) Why is the crust under the oceans different from that of the continents? (3) How permanent are the ocean basins?

Of, course, when we have discovered the complete answer to all of these questions, we will have also unraveled the complete history of the Earth. At present, the best we can do is to point to some significant facts about the Earth which indicate the most fruitful lines of exploration.

Where Did the Water Come from?

Water, air, and life (composing respectively, the hydrosphere, the atmosphere, and the biosphere) are made up of elements that are not abundant in the lithosphere or even in volcanic rocks derived from deep within the Earth. Consequently, any question that we ask about the source of the water in the oceans might as well be asked about the chloride ion in sea water, carbon dioxide and nitrogen in the air, and organic compounds in animals and plants. For all these compounds originate somehow other than by the weathering of igneous rocks.

To understand the origin of these materials at the surface of the Earth we must turn to the general features of the Solar System, for that is where the clues are hidden. The Sun, other planets, and the extraterrestrial material we recover as meteorites can tell us much about the history of the oceans.

Since 95 per cent of the mass of the Solar System is in the Sun, we logically expect that the primitive nebula from which the Sun and Solar System formed must have had approximately the same composition as that of the Sun. When we consider the abundances, relative to silicon, of the elements estimated for the whole Solar System (Table 7–1), we see that some elements are deficient in the Earth compared to the Sun (or the Solar System as a whole). This is particularly evident in the depletion of the very unreactive gases—neon, argon, krypton, and xenon, the so-called "noble" gases (Fig. 7–1).

Other elements that formed volatile (or gaseous) phases in great abundance in the primitive nebula would also be strongly depleted of solid particles during the process of planetary accumulation. Hence water vapor, hydrogen chloride gas, carbon dioxide, carbon monoxide or methane, and nitrogen or ammonia gas would not be included in the growing Earth. Only the nonvolatile compounds of chlorine, carbon, hydrogen, and nitrogen would accummulate during the formation of the Earth. Water in clay-type minerals and other hydrated silicate minerals, carbon in organic compounds with low boiling points, nitrogen in ammonium ions included in the lattice of potassium-bearing minerals, and chlorine as ions substituting for the oxygen atoms in silicates or occurring as rare chloride minerals—these are the forms that would have permitted accumulation of elements which mainly formed volatile compounds in the primitive nebula. All of these compounds have been found in certain meteorites, known as the *carbonaceous chondrites* (Fig. 7–2), which appear to satisfy the

FIGURE 7–1 *The rare-gases (Ne, Ar, Kr, and Xe) are depleted on Earth compared to "cosmic" abundances when silicon is used for normalization implying that Earth did not retain a large primitive atmosphere during its initial condensation. Only molecules existing in nonvolatile compounds were accreted with the solid particles and were later able to escape to the surface to form the Earth's atmosphere. (From H. Brown, in* The Atmospheres of the Earth and Planets, *ed. by G. Kuiper, U. of Chicago Press, 1952.)*

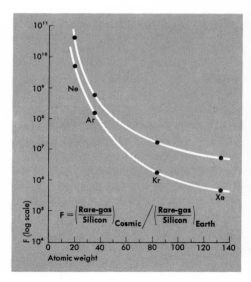

Table 7–1

Composition of the Solar System*

Atomic Number	Element	Primitive Solar System	Sun	Atomic Number	Element	Primitive Solar System	Sun
1	H	3.2×10^{10}	3.2×10^{10}	44	Ru	1.58	.93
2	He	2.6×10^{9}		45	Rh	.26	.19
3	Li	38	.29	46	Pd	1.00	.51
4	Be	7	7.2	47	Ag	.26	.044
5	B	6		48	Cd	.89	.91
6	C	1.66×10^{7}	1.66×10^{7}	49	In	.11	.46
7	N	3.0×10^{6}	3.0×10^{6}	50	Sn	1.33	1.10
8	O	2.9×10^{7}	2.9×10^{7}	51	Sb	.15	2.8
9	F	$\sim 10^{3}$		52	Te	3.00	
10	Ne	2.9×10^{6}		53	I	.46	
11	Na	4.18×10^{4}	6.3×10^{4}	54	Xe	3.15	
12	Mg	1.046×10^{6}	7.9×10^{5}	55	Cs	.25	
13	Al	8.93×10^{4}	5.0×10^{4}	56	Ba	4.0	4.0
14	Si	1.00×10^{6}	1.00×10^{6}	57	La	.38	
15	P	9320	6900	58	Ce	1.08	
16	S	6.0×10^{5}	6.3×10^{5}	59	Pr	.16	
17	Cl	1836		60	Nd	.69	
18	Ar	2.4×10^{5}		62	Sm	.24	
19	K	2970	1580	63	Eu	.083	
20	Ca	7.28×10^{4}	4.5×10^{4}	64	Gd	.33	
21	Sc	29	21	65	Tb	.054	
22	Ti	3140	1510	66	Dy	.33	
23	V	590	158	67	Ho	.076	
24	Cr	1.20×10^{4}	5000	68	Er	.21	
25	Mn	6320	2500	69	Tm	.032	
26	Fe	8.50×10^{4}	1.17×10^{5}	70	Yb	.18	1.07
27	Co	750	1380	71	Lu	.031	
28	Ni	1.5×10^{4}	2.6×10^{4}	72	Hf	.16	
29	Cu	39	3500	73	Ta	.021	
30	Zn	202	800	74	W	.11	
31	Ga	9.05	7.2	75	Re	.054	
32	Ge	134	62	76	Os	.73	
33	As	4.4		77	Ir	.500	
34	Se	18.8		78	Pt	1.157	
35	Br	3.95		79	Au	.13	
36	Kr	20		80	Hg	.27	
37	Rb	5.0	9.5	81	Tl	.11	
38	Sr	21	13.5	82	Pb	2.2	2.5
39	Y	3.6	5.6	83	Bi	.14	
40	Zr	23	54	90	Th	.069	
41	Nb	.81	2.8	92	U	.042	
42	Mo	2.42	2.5				

After Cameron, 1966, in *Handbook of Physical Constants*, ed. by S. P. Clark, Geological Society of America.

* Listed as the number of atoms per 10^6 atoms of silicon.

requirements for at least some of the material forming the Earth.

As was implied above, the weathering of crustal rocks will not yield the excess chlorine, water, carbon dioxide, and nitrogen found in the hydrosphere, atmosphere, and biosphere as well as that tied up in sedimentary rocks. These elements and their compounds have thus been called "excess volatiles" by W. W. Rubey who has estimated their abundance on the Earth's surface (Table 7–2). It is apparent that the "excess volatiles," rather than condensing from the primitive nebula during planet formation, were derived from the Earth's interior by degassing, after the Earth was formed. There are two possible ways the derivation from the interior could have occurred: The Earth could have undergone some radical thermal metamorphosis at which time it spewed out the volatile components now composing the hydrosphere, atmosphere, and biosphere; or the degassing of the Earth's interior could be a continuous process whereby the abundance of "excess volatiles" on the surface is slowly increasing as the result of volcanic action. Although scientists sway from one extreme to the other, there is as yet no unequivocal evidence for the choice of one theory over the other.

FIGURE 7–2 *This is a piece of a meteorite that was observed to fall at Orgueil, France on May 14, 1864. It is a typical carbonaceous chondrite, containing organic compounds, clay-like minerals, and an assemblage of other minerals which seem to indicate a complex origin. Many scientists think that this type of meteorite resembles one kind of material from which the Earth and other planets were formed. It provides the necessary carbon to reduce iron to a metal phase as seen in some meteorites and inferred to compose the core of the Earth. (Courtesy U.S. National Museum.)*

The reasons for this ambiguity are twofold: (1) The age of the Earth, as inferred from meteorites, is 4.5 billion years, whereas the oldest rocks dated on the Earth are 3.2 billion years old; therefore, we have no record of events during the first 1.3 billion years of the Earth's history. The sedimentary rocks of this early period, if preserved, would have been an important source of information for the testing of the consequences of one model or the other.

Table 7–2

"Excess Volatiles" *

Substance	Units of 10^{20} Grams
Water	16,600
Total carbon as carbon dioxide	910
Chlorine	300
Nitrogen	42
Sulfur	22

After Rubey (1951), reprinted in Brancazio and Cameron, 1964.

* In the atmosphere, hydrosphere, and buried sedimentary rocks.

(2) We have no clearcut evidence for the derivation of volatiles from the deep interior of the Earth (the mantle) by way of volcanoes, fumaroles, and hot springs. On the basis of chemical tests, the volatiles sampled can be explained as the result of the inclusion of sediments, ground water, or sea water. Hence, the test for present-day degassing from the mantle is impossible to make and must be assumed on the basis of other hunches.

Following are statements of the arguments for both early and continuous degassing of the Earth.

Early Degassing

We do not have a sample of the material from which the Earth itself was formed, so we must depend on using, as a first approximation, material arriving on our planet from other parts of our Solar System in the form of meteorites. Meteorites were not subjected to the complex history typical of crustal rocks, and thus in their number we should find closer analogs to primitive planetary material than we do on the Earth There are a wide range of meteoritic types, but one type in particular is of interest for our present discussion. These are the carbonaceous chondrites mentioned above. Some fraction of the accumulating Earth must have been composed of material very much like that which we find in carbonaceous chondrites. Many carbonaceous chondrites are composed of low-boiling-point organic compounds, hydrated silicates similar to the clay mineral chlorite, and iron oxide, as well as some other silicates and easily soluble salts. If this material were heated up by the gravitational heat of accumulation or by the energy released by short-lived radioactive nuclides extant in the early years of our Solar System, the water would be released from the hydrated minerals and the iron oxide and iron-bearing silicates would be reduced to form metallic iron and probably carbon monoxide. These and associated compounds would form the raw materials for the air, oceans, and ultimately life. The heating, the formation of metallic iron and segregation of the Earth's iron core, and the release of the excess volatiles and of salts easily dissolved by the vapors would cause degassing in the first 500 million years of the Earth's existence. This single episodic event would be compatible with all that we know about the other constituents of the Earth's atmosphere and the nature of the ancient rocks.

Continual Degassing

If no episodic event occurred as described above early in the history of the Earth, then the "excess volatiles" could be accreting at the Earth's surface by degassing of water and other components from the mantle over geologic time. What are the indications of this? We know that heat flows outward from the interior of the Earth and that the process locally generates volcanic material. It is not inconceivable that some "excess volatiles" are also released at the time of volcanic eruptions. Although it is impossible to ascertain whether any of the gaseous material in volcanoes or fumaroles or hot springs is newly derived from the mantle, it has been determined by Rubey that only 1 per cent of the present rate of volatile supply by volcanoes need be from the mantle throughout the history of the Earth to produce the oceans and the atmosphere.

We cannot choose between these two options with present data, but perhaps information from the other planets will permit us to rewrite the history of ocean water sometime in the near future.

Continental and Oceanic Crusts

The differences between the oceanic crust and the continental crust lie in thickness and composition. The continental surface rocks are granitic and metamorphic rocks with high silica content to a large degree, whereas the oceanic surface rocks are basaltic (low in silica). The depth, measured from sea level, to the Mohorovičić discontinuity (the seismically determined boundary between mantle and crust) is about 40 kilometers under the continents and 11 kilometers under the oceans. The total mass to the center of the Earth per unit of surface area is the same for both oceanic and continental areas although the mass distribution near the surface of the Earth is different, as shown in Fig. 7–3.

With these bits of information about the continental oceanic crusts, we can propose an explanation for the existence of continents and oceans. The continents are the areas of concentration of the rocks of lower density compared to those of the oceanic crust. The low-density rocks like granite are also the equivalent in composition to the first molten fraction that is formed during the heating of a variety of silicate rocks, including sediments. This process is enhanced in the presence of water. Since the deeper we go in the Earth the hotter it gets, sediments depressed sufficiently will undergo partial melting. The low-melting fraction, resem-

FIGURE 7–3 *A representation of the crusts under land and sea. The mass in each column from 0 to 33 km is the same. Geophysicists have used these as "adopted standard sections," but locally, more detailed columns have been constructed. (After Worzel and Shurbet, 1955, in Crust of the Earth, ed. by Poldevaart.)*

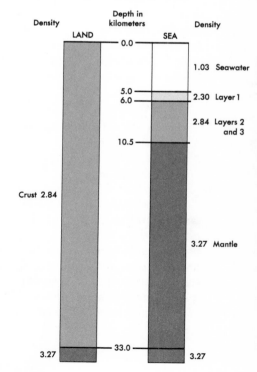

bling some continental igneous and metamorphic rocks, will gradually be displaced upward because its density is lower than that of the residue. The radioactive elements, uranium, thorium and potassium are carried with this material. The result is a higher heat-producing capability at the surface of continents compared to a lower heat-producing capability deep under the continents.

Once the nucleus of a continent is formed, subsequent weathering of the rocks, the resulting sedimentation, and ultimate metamorphism by heating during continental mountain-building continue the process of continent generation (or regeneration) around the primitive continental nucleus. The margins of the continents play a significant role in the process in that they represent the major sites of sediment accumulation and are subject to structural weaknesses resulting in the supply of new material from the mantle, sediment-trapping, mountain-building, and metamorphism. The distribution of radioactive ages in the rocks of North America (Fig. 7–4) seem to indicate such an accretionary history. Other continents, however, do not show this simple pattern indicating that the actual histories of the continents are more complex.

The Mobility of Ocean Basins

We have evidence of movement of the continental crust—by displacements observed during earthquakes, in the existence of mountains, and in highly distorted sedimentary rocks. Until recently the mobility of the ocean floor was inferred primarily from sedimentologic and topographic observations although earthquake activity had been recorded, particularly along the oceanic ridge systems. Magnetic surveys over the oceans supply more direct evidence of the nature of ocean-floor mobility. Let us consider each of the arguments.

Sediment Age and Thickness

The oldest sediments sampled from the deep sea are Cretaceous in age; that is, they are no more than 100 million years old. The ancient sediments are exposed in areas of slumping or erosion by bottom-scouring currents. Since we do find a range of sediments from the recent past back to Cretaceous time, it is surprising that older sediments are not encountered.

Using thicknesses of sediments, as obtained by seismic reflection methods and rates of accumulation obtained by radioactive geochronometry, we can establish the amount of time required for all the sediment to accumulate at any point in the ocean. We assume when we do this that the rate of the last several hundred thousand years was also the rate throughout geologic time. The results indicate that along the Mid-Atlantic Ridge the sediments veneering the sea mounts are about 50 meters deep on the average. At an accumulation rate of 1 centimeter of sediment (carbonate and clay) in 1,000 years it would take

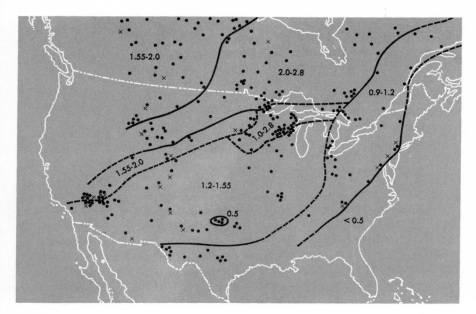

FIGURE 7–4 *Radioactive ages in billions of years, on granites and metamorphic rocks (i.e., rocks transformed from other rock types by heat and pressure and commonly found in terranes containing granitic rocks) from the central part of North America. The dots fall within the age ranges of the boundaries while the crosses do not. The pattern indicates some sort of zonal structure that may be due to continental growth with time or some other major types of zonal alteration. (After Tilton and Hart, 1963.)*

5 million years to provide the measured thickness. This is compatible with the potassium-argon ages of basaltic boulders dredged from the same area, ages that range from less than 1 million years up to about 5 million years.

In the Argentine basin where the sediment thickness is 3,000 meters, the rate of accumulation is about 6 centimeters in 1,000 years. This rate means that 50 million years would be required to accumulate the thickest section of deep-sea sediments found to date in the oceans.

It is evident that soft sediments which have distinctive seismic reflection properties and which can be penetrated by deep-sea coring tubes represent a sediment record younger than 100 million years. Since the Earth is 4.5 billion years old, this figure is only 2 per cent of geologic time. Any earlier record in the ocean must be either so diminutive as to have been missed, transformed by lithification, obscured by volcanic debris, or swept under the continents by a highly mobile ocean bottom. Let us examine these alternatives in greater detail:

1. The rates of accumulation were much slower before the glacial age. This explanation is not now generally acceptable because potassium-argon dating of volcanic layers in the sediments indicates no major discontinuity in accumulation rates as far back as 30 million years, long before the glacial age began.

2. The sediments, as they accumulate, are compacted to form a dense phase which, along with volcanic rocks, constitute Layer 2, the "basement layer"

The history of oceans and ocean basins

(see Table 1–1). If this were the case, then the depth to the "basement layer" should be about the same in all parts of the ocean. The 3,000 meters of uncompacted sediment that fill the rugged topography of the Argentine basin seems to rule out this explanation as a general one.

3. There are three processes operating to determine the thickness of soft sediments at any point in the ocean: rate of deposition, scouring by bottom currents and slumping, and lava flows covering the sediments. All three processes have been seen to be effective, singly, at points on the ocean bottom, and it is not inconceivable that their combined action could give the range of thickness and structure observed in the deep-sea sediments. Some of the debris would have to be found in the abyssal plains if this were generally the case.

4. The ocean floor sediments are transported under the continents as the result of ocean-floor spreading. This explanation is particularly attractive in light of the recent interpretation of magnetic anomolies in the deep ocean, a topic which is discussed below.

Ocean-Bottom Topography

The ocean-bottom topography shows strong linear trends of ridges. Areas like the Mid-Atlantic Ridge and the East Pacific Rise are sites of seismic activity and of volcanism. A "fossil" ridge area called the Darwin Rise has been located in the western Pacific Ocean. This is demarked by submarine flat-topped sea-mounts with a maximum depth of 1,600 meters to the tops. The flat tops give evidence of weathering and erosion by the presence of oxidized iron, and indicate shallow water by the presence of shells of shallow-water organisms. Evidently these volcanic cones were once exposed above sea level, as the islands of the South Pacific are now, but have subsided since the Cretaceous period about 100 million years ago. The extent of this ancient rise indicates large-scale vertical movements on the ocean floor.

There are also evidences for east-west breaks and for displacements of several hundred kilometers both in the Atlantic and the Pacific, indicating mobility of the ocean bottom. The effects are comparable to those found on land in such places as California where the San Andreas fault is the major source of large-scale lateral movements and the cause of intense earthquakes.

The Mid-Atlantic Ridge, which is just about in the middle of the ocean, has trend features that approximate those of the continents to the east and west of it. Most strikingly, it appears as if South America and Africa could almost be fitted together, with the mid-Atlantic Ridge as the "seam."

Magnetic-Anomaly Patterns

In Chapter 4 we discussed the fact that the Earth's magnetic field reverses itself periodically. This well-dated phenomenon can be applied to the problem of ocean-bottom mobility.

As has been noted earlier, the major oceanic ridge systems are sites of volcanic activity as well as seismic activity. We know that when a lava flow begins to crystalize on the Earth's surface, the magnetic minerals respond to the magnetic polarity at the time of extrusion. The magnetization is sufficiently strong to survive the vicissitudes of geologic time as long as the temperature is not raised too high again or major chemical alteration does not take place. Lava flows, then, act as a record of the changing magnetic polarity of the Earth. Although clearly oriented volcanic rock samples on land have been used to document the changing polarity of the last 4 million years, such an approach is not possible for submarine volcanic material. Dredging volcanic rock samples from the bottom of the sea gives no information on orientation.

A sensitive magnetometer, measuring the Earth's magnetic intensity, towed by a ship or airplane is able to sense the small variations in magnetic intensity over local magnetic bodies such as volcanic rocks. If the magnets have formed in the Earth's present-day polarity, they reinforce the magnetic effect measured by the magnetometer, whereas if the polarity was reversed at the time of the solidification of the lava, the present-day magnetic intensity is subtracted from by the small reversely oriented magnets. Either of these effects result in so called "magnetic anomalies."

Surveys of the major oceanic ridge systems have revealed symmetrical magnetic-anomaly patterns which are attributed to the processes described above (Fig. 7–5). However, the symmetrical pattern around the center of the ridge implies that if the major volcanic activity has been happening at the crests, then the ridges must be pulling apart to allow the recording of new events by even younger submarine lava flows. From magnetic-anomaly patterns, that can be related directly to known magnetic reversals, it has been calculated that the ridges are separating from either side of the crest at the rate of from 1 centimeter per year (southern Mid-Atlantic Ridge) to 4.5 centimeters per year (southern East Pacific Rise).

This observation is the clearest single evidence for the fact that the ocean floors are highly mobile and indeed spreading away from the ridges toward the continental margins.

There have been several theories to explain these observations. As is common in attempts at scientific explanations, at some point a presupposition is made about the fundamental mechanism which then allows the pieces of data to be interpreted in its framework.

One of the most productive models is that the ocean bottoms are regenerated by the action of convection currents within the mantle. These currents actually transport old ocean bottom away from the ridges, which are the places where the mantle material rises (Fig. 7–5). The lateral transport away from the ridge-area pulls the continents apart as well. In the Atlantic this movement would explain the similar patterns of the west coast of Africa, the east coast of South America, and the Mid-Atlantic Ridge. The convection cells, which move at the rate of 1 cm/year, last from 100 to 200 million years. The continents

The history of oceans and ocean basins

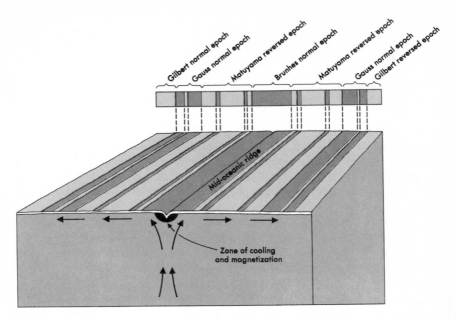

FIGURE 7-5 *Magnetic anomalies form symmetrical patterns about the axes of the major ridge systems. These may be interpreted as due to the reinforcement and subtraction of magnetic intensity locally because of magnets oriented in the direction of the present field and in the reverse direction respectively. If this interpretation is valid it explains the excellent correlation between the magnetic reversal intervals and the geographic dimensions of the anomaly patterns as the result of constant rates of spreading of the ocean floor at a particular location. The spreading is associated with new submarine flows in which magnetic orientations reflect the field at the time of emplacement. The cause of the spreading may be due to slow-moving convection cells in the upper mantle. (From "Reversals of the Earth's Magnetic Field," Cox, Dalrymple, and Doell. Copyright © 1967 by Scientific American, Inc. All rights reserved.)*

respond to the movements by contracting at their margins during mountain-formation, incorporating not only nearshore sediments but portions of the older parts of the sea floor. By this regenerative action the ocean bottoms appear to be relatively young at all times. These ideas have been espoused and developed by many scientists but most persistently by H. H. Hess, R. Dietz, and J. T. Wilson.

It is certain that no explanation for the observed properties of the ocean bottom will ever be so well founded as to require no difficult presuppositions. There are, however, important tests yet to be made in the study of the ocean floor. Perhaps the most important of these is deeper penetration of the ocean bottom by coring devices. Programs for obtaining cores penetrating to 1,000 meters have been shown to be feasible, and useful data will be obtained from these long cores in the near future. In addition, the program for penetrating through the entire oceanic crust (the *Mohole*) will undoubtedly also be consummated as soon as interest and technology permit.

Appendix

Conversion factors

Fathom (fm) = 6 feet (ft) = 1.829 meters (m)
Meter (m) = 100 centimeters (cm) = 39.37 inches (in) = 3.281 ft
Kilometer (km) = 0.6214 miles (mi)
Micron (μ) = 10^{-6} m = 10^{-4} cm
Centimeters per second (cm/sec.) = 0.0360 km/hr. = 0.0224 mi/hr
Liter (l) = 1000 cm^3 = 10^{-3} m^3 = 1.057 quarts
Kilogram (kg) = 10^3 grams (g) = 2.205 pounds (lb)
Microgram (μg) = 10^{-6} g
Year = 31,560,000 seconds
2.303 log (base 10)x = ln (base e or natural base) x

Constants

Avogadro's Number = 6.023 $\times$ 10^{23} g^{-1} mole^{-1} (molecule per gram-molecular weight)
Universal Gravitational Constant = 6.670 $\times$ 10^{-8} dynes cm^2 g^{-2}
π = 3.1416
e = 2.7182

Terrestrial constants

Mass of the Earth = 5.976 $\times$ 10^{27} g
Area of the Earth = 510.100 $\times$ 10^6 km^2
Equatorial radius of the Earth = 6378.163 km
Polar radius of the Earth = 6356.177 km
Area of the oceans = 362.033 $\times$ 10^6 km^2
Mean depth of the oceans = 3729 m
Volume of the oceans = 1.350 $\times$ 10^9 km^3
Volume of the Earth = 1.083 $\times$ 10^{12} km^3
Standard acceleration of free fall on Earth = 980.665 cm sec.$^{-2}$

Suggestions for further reading and bibliography

General

Brancazio, P. J., and A. G. W. Cameron (*Eds.*) *The Origin and Evolution of Atmospheres and Oceans*. New York: Wiley, 1964.

Defant, A., *Physical Oceanography, Volume 1 and 2*. Oxford: Pergamon, 1960.

Dietrich, G., *General Oceanography*. New York: Interscience (Wiley), 1963.

Garrels, R. M., and C. L. Christ, *Solutions, Minerals and Equilibria*. New York: Harper and Row, 1965.

Heezen, B. C., M. Tharp and M. Ewing, *The Floors of the Oceans, I: The North Atlantic*. Boulder, Colorado: The Geological Society of America, 1959.

Hill, M. N. (*ed.*), *The Sea, Volume 1, 2 and 3*. New York: Interscience (Wiley), 1962.

King, C. A. M., *An Introduction to Oceanography*. New York: McGraw-Hill, 1963.

Krauskopf, K. B., *Introduction to Geochemistry*. New York: McGraw-Hill, 1967.

Mason, B., *Principles of Geochemistry*. New York: Wiley, 1966.

Menard, H. W., *Marine Geology of the Pacific*. New York: McGraw-Hill, 1964.

Pickard, G. L., *Descriptive Physical Oceanography*. Oxford: Pergamon, 1963.

Poldervaart, A. (*Ed.*) *Crust of the Earth*. Boulder, Colorado: The Geological Society of America, 1955.

Riley, J. P. and G. Skirrow (*eds.*), *Chemical Oceanography, Volume 1 and 2*. London and New York: Academic Press, 1965.

Sears, M. (*ed.*), *Oceanography*. Washington: American Association for the Advancement of Science, 1961.

Stommel, H., *The Gulf Stream*. Berkeley, Calif.: University of California, 1958.

Sverdrup, H. U., M. W. Johnson and R. H. Fleming, *The Oceans*. Englewood Cliffs, New Jersey: Prentice-Hall, 1942.

Von Arx, W. S., *An Introduction to Physical Oceanography*. Reading, Mass.: Addison-Wesley, 1962.

Topography and structure

Drake, C. L., M. Ewing, and G. H. Sutton, *Physics and Chemistry of the Earth*, 3, 110–198 Pergamon, (1959).

Ewing, M., J. I. Ewing, and M. Talwani, *Geol. Soc. Am. Bull.*, 75, 17–36 (1964).

Ewing, M., W. J. Ludwig, and J. I. Ewing, *Jour. Geophys. Res.*, 69, 2003–2032 (1964).

Hill, M. M., *Physics and Chemistry of the Earth*, 2, 129–163, Pergamon, (1957).

Talwani, M., X. L. LePichon, and M. Ewing, *Jour. Geophys. Res.*, 70, 341–352 (1965).

Talwani, M., G. H. Sutton, and J. L. Worzel, *Jour. Geophys. Res.*, 64, 1545–1555 (1959).

Rona, P. A., and C. S. Clay, *Jour. Geophys. Res.*, 72, 2107–2130 (1967).

Sedimentary deposits

Biscaye, P. E., *Geol. Soc. Am. Bull.*, 76, 803–832, (1965).

Bonatti, E., *Trans. New York Acad. Sci.*, 25, 938–948, (1963).

Delany, A. C., Audrey C. Delany, D. W. Parkin, J. J. Griffin, E. D. Goldberg, and B. E. F. Reimann, *Geochim, et Cosmochim. Acta*, 31, 885–909, (1967)

Heezen, B. C. and C. L. Drake, *Am. Assoc. Petro. Geol. Bull.*, 48, 221–225, (1964).

Heezen, B. C., and C. Hollister, *Marine Geol.*, 1, 141–174, (1964).

Mero, J. L., Manganese nodules on the ocean floor, *Institute of Marine Resources, Dept. Mineral Technology, Univ. of Calif.*, (1961).

Skornyakova, N.S. and P. F. Andruschenko, *Lithology and Useful Minerals* (*Akad. Nauk USSR*), 21–36, (1964).

Turekian, K. K. and J. Imbrie, *Earth and Planetary Sci. Letters*, 1, 161–168, (1966).

Stratigraphy and geochronometry

Broecker, W. S., K. K. Turekian, and B. C. Heezen, *Am. Jour. Sci.*, 256, 503–517, (1958).

Cox, A., G. B. Dalrymple, and R. R. Doell, *Scientific American*, 216, Feb., (1967).

Dymond, J. R., *Science*, 152, 1239–1241, (1966).

Emiliani, C., *Jour. Geol.*, 63, 538–578, (1955).

Ericson, D. B., M. Ewing, G. Wollin, and B. C. Heezen, *Geol. Soc. Am. Bull.*, 72, 193–286, (1961).

Ku, T.-L. and W. S. Broecker, *Science*, 151, 448–450, (1966).

Ninkovich, D. and B. C. Heezen, *Nature*, 213, 582–584, (1967).

Opdyke, N. D., B. Glass, J. D. Hays, and J. Foster, *Science*, 154, 349–357, (1966).

Tilton, G. R. and S. R. Hart, *Science*, 140, 357–366, (1963).

Ocean water

Duursma, E. K., *Netherlands Jour. Sea Res.*, 1, 1–147, (1961).

Knauss, J. A., *Jour. Geophys. Res.*, 67, 3943–3954, (1962).

Schutz, D. F. and K. K. Turekian, *Jour. Geophys. Res.*, 70, 5519–5528, (1965).

Index